"backwards!"

Remember, when times
get hard... Look up!

31 May 18

SEARCH YOUR THOUGHTS
THIS IS WAR

CALVIN L. REED

Part I – SEARCH

Part II –THOUGHTS

- There are no mistakes in God's great plan of life.
- God gave us a gift called "emotional feelings."
- Negative emotions bring on a negative mood.
- God granted us the ability to choose the images we want to think about and dwell upon in our minds.
- Many have a hard time realizing that our thoughts bring action.
- Our belief systems stem from how we evaluate something.

Part III – WAR

- The devil sets us up.
- Never forget that we are always in battle with the enemy.
- To combat darts from the enemy, we have to be concerned with what's acceptable to God.
- Satan can't handle positive thoughts.
- So the next question for you is: how badly do you want your freedom?
- Sometimes you might have a pity party, but try not to stay at the party too long.
- Sometimes even our foundational process for developing a relationship with Christ begins with deception from the enemy.

- Put your confidence in Jesus.
- You have to know fear and doubt will come.
- Remember strange storms always precede great miracles.
- We have to look for the supernatural.
- Too many times we believe in God's word enough to encourage others, but don't believe His promises apply to us.
- We must think and speak in agreement with God, and believe it will be.
- What is your normal mind when your mind is renewed?
- Understand that your mind aids your spirit.
- God is ALWAYS in the business of teaching principles of discipline.
- We have to practice taking action and making ourselves aware of the problems.
- I know this is a lot to take in, just don't let unbelief and doubt steal your peace.
- Our words are very important. We speak things into existence.
- God will deal with your strongholds before your behavior can change.
- If you don't resist people's wrong thoughts, you often will take them as your own thoughts.
- The old you died to Christ, and now you are new.
- We have to give God praise now.
- Continually saying "What if" brings on fear and negative thinking.
- Many will say that slumps occur for different reasons.
- We have to SEARCH our THOUGHTS, because this is WAR.

I dedicate this book to my big homie Jesus, the realest God I know, and my wonderful and supportive family, especially the two women that were instrumental in my success, my wife Jenn and my mom. With this supporting cast surrounding me, how can I not win?

I would like to acknowledge my heavenly Father, Jesus. I once read, while He walked this earth:

- He was loving, but didn't let His compassion immobilize Him.
- He didn't have a bloated ego, even though He was often surrounded by adoring crowds.
- He maintained balance despite an often demanding lifestyle.
- He always knew what He was doing and where He was going.
- He cared deeply about people, including women and children (they weren't considered important back then).
- He was able to accept people while not merely winking at their sin.
- He responded to individuals based on where they were and what they uniquely needed.
- He stayed true to the principles stated above.

I pray I can learn from such a great God. He's so Big Time! I also would like to acknowledge ALL the staff at Xulon Press Christian Publishing, but specifically their publishing consultant Michelle Johnston. If it were not for her bubbly spirit and wealth of knowledge that helped my fears to subside, you would not be reading this book today. She was the first vessel that God used to pull this mission to completion. Thank you, my sister!

MY FIRST "TRUE" BOOK REVIEW

Dear Mr. Reed:

I **wanted to share with you the wonderful impact that your book, although still just in manuscript form, has already had on my life.**

I have OCD. Not major OCD, but enough that I get so wrapped up and lost in my thoughts that sometimes it's a daily struggle to escape from them. Your book has truly inspired me to turn those thoughts and those worries to God. It's not going to be an easy path, but if you could do it, through incarceration and military service, then certainly so can I!

I also have a hard time accepting anything outside of what I believe to be "right," and because of that, it can take me a long time to make positive changes in my life. I'm one of the many cookie-cutter Christians to whom your book speaks—my communion with God consists largely of church-going, rituals, and by-the-book prayer. I might stop to say a quick word to the Lord sometimes, but I ALWAYS bracket it with a "Father, Son, Holy Spirit" while crossing myself, before and after I pray.

Reading about how God speaks to us in many different ways, not just through the bible and through the church, really struck a chord with me. I thought, maybe this book is the way He has chosen to reach me. He knows that if someone handed me a published book, I might be skeptical to read it, wondering why it was different, why that particular book applies to my life. But editing is my passion, and He spoke to me through my passion—through editing your manuscript.

Although I've been told this numerous times before, it wasn't until I saw some of the literally life-changing examples in your book that I realized just how present God is in our everyday lives, and how much He wants us to have a constant dialogue with Him. Driving home after my first day of working on your manuscript, I passed an absolutely horrible car accident. I then did something I never did before— without bowing my head, crossing myself, or stopping the car to kneel, I just spoke a few words, "God, please be with those people and their families right now in their time of need." That was it—so simple. It felt great!

I want to thank you for your inspiring words. I know I'm just the first of many that this book will touch, and I am eager to see what other improvements it makes in my life. Thank you for sharing your stories with the world, to help others like me make positive changes. God Bless You!

Warm Regards,
Natasha

Part I

SEARCH

———⊗⊗⊗———

How dear is a friend to whom we can pour out our hearts, knowing we will not be cast away. Jesus is our friend!

Of late, God has had me minister to numerous people, whom He has sent to me, about His will for their life. The constant theme among the group is the struggle to understand what God wants them to do. Some have cried out their hearts to God and feel that He doesn't hear them, due to His lack of response. Others feel that they hear his response, but can't complete what He requires of them. Most just feel that they aren't worthy of His answer, yet they continue to ask Him questions. So God inspired me to take all of these conversations and relay them in manuscript form: hence the book you are reading right now.

My life has been a crazy roller coaster since my conception, and sometimes I feel like I shouldn't be the one giving ANYBODY advice. Then I think about the life of Saul in the bible. He was a killer: he was charged by the government to kill anybody that followed the faith. He was enthused to complete this task that would seem grotesque to most. Even though believers had the covering of God over their life, they were still fearful of this mortal man. He had some-thing that many won't ever receive in their lifetime: he had the ability to commit to something that he believed in. He believed in murdering followers of Christ and committed to it wholeheartedly, to the point that he traveled afar, actively searching for these individuals. In our time, we would say he shared a mindset kindred to a gang member. He was down for his set affiliation at all costs. If you can't visualize that, we can say he resembled a soldier in the United States Army that was tasked to deploy to a foreign land and kill the enemy. He didn't know these individuals or anything about them. He didn't care. He just did his job and went home satisfied.

When I hear the story of Saul spoken by fellow brothers and sisters in the faith, it seems they always focus on the transformation of Saul to Paul on the road to Damascus as if God changed him from being evil to righteous, like an aston-ishing magic trick happened. Think about this though: God made Saul the same way He made you and me. He knew the type of man that Saul was inwardly. He knew Saul was about the cause, and that he wasn't shaky. A man that can kill another man with no remorse is a man that can withstand the ridicule and hatred from his fellow men as he speaks about the greatness of his Savior. God knew what the others couldn't see in Saul. So to me, all Saul was lacking was the revelation. He needed a true reason to worship God besides someone just verbalizing it to him out of his or her mouth. That revelation request, even though it wasn't verbalized per se by Saul, still wasn't beyond something that God could do. Once Saul saw the light, God knew he would go to the ends of the earth to spread the gospel to people seeking the truth the same way he had sought out believers to kill them.

As I contemplate that message over and over in my brain, the Holy Spirit says, "That's you, C.J." See, I am a truth seeker. This truth is not limited to the Word of God, but truth in general. I am the type of person to never take an individual's words at face value. Even if I know you are right, I will still check in some way to verify. That's just me. To the natural eye, I might not be the visual representation you would hope to see when you think of a believer that is intimately in love with Christ. I'm tatted up. I tend to slip up and curse every now and then. I might get upset and spazz on someone that doesn't deserve it. Even though I'm married, you might catch me lustful for a moment and staring at another female's breasts longer than I should. I am aware of all this within myself, but at the end of the day, I'm me. I work daily to kill the old me, and I praise God for where He has taken me from my past experiences. If you turned your nose up to any of those things I noted, I'm glad you didn't meet me years ago. You would have doused me in a bathtub of holy water like I was an extra in the movie *The Exorcist*. Yet even with the wild life that I lived, I have the ability to commit. This is the reason I have walked in faith and completed this book.

I know that there is a spirit of renewing and everlasting change attached to this piece of work. Romans 10:17 says, "So then faith comes by hearing, and hearing by the word of God." If you are reading this, it is a divine appointment in your life. Though I may ask God, "Why me?" when referring to writing this book, like you, I too shall BE BOLD and commit to His divine appointment for my life. For a teacher cannot teach without gaining some type of perspective for himself, because the lesson of life is forever evolving under the great care of our Creator. So we both will use this as a time of learning and not just teaching!

Part II

THOUGHTS

I n 2006, I remember being approached by my friends with a book and DVD called, *The Secret*. Many are familiar with both, so I won't go into extensive detail about them. *The Secret* is based upon the law of attraction. The law of attraction, in a nutshell, says that "like attracts like." It's the belief that positive thinking can bring reward to your life. It will create results such as grand wealth, supernatural health, and overall happiness. That book alone sold over 19 million copies worldwide, so there is definitely a want for it among consumers.

I was also curious, so I watched the DVD with my friends. The entire time, their eyes were stretched as far as they could go. They soaked in every drop of information as if it were an unspoken key to life. I agreed with many of the points noted within the DVD, but from a different perspective. I felt they had taken a portion of biblical truth and fed it to the masses as a "get rich quick" scheme to exploit it. What do I mean when I say exploit? I mean they promised us a destination, but they didn't give us a proper vehicle to get us there.

So here I stand to speak about the truth of thoughts, and the war that Satan is waging within them. The creators of *The Secret* knew that all people want to be wealthy, healthy, and happy all the time. Who doesn't? They promised a step-by-step process that would create these things. That process is half true. If I work at CVS as a photo station clerk, but deep down I want to be a world-renowned surgeon, then yes, I have to see it first. We all have to visualize ourselves being whatever it is we want to be. That applies, regardless if our mental picture is positive or negative. To be a great police officer or a great drug dealer, you have to see yourself in that role. That's how powerful our minds are. If you continue to see yourself in a certain light, then you will eventually accept it as truth. So, in that respect, *The Secret* was correct.

What I want to clarify is that this process has many of us just auto-suggesting a better life. When times get tough, we fall back into our "happy thoughts," as if they alone will bring us closer to the Promised Land. There is more required. That more is called hard work, along with the guidance of the Holy Spirit. I can't just visualize that one day I will be a surgeon, and think that it will happen solely based upon that visual. I have to get up and move on the thought.

As a believer, I also include God as I make my decisions to go attain my goals. *The Secret* is based upon the natural law of the universe. Even though that sounds out of this world, I am still forced to look up at the God who created the universe. How can I just listen to the law of attraction, as if God has no control over my life? Many of you reading probably are asking yourself the question, "Well I don't understand why I can't follow both *The Secret* and God's words." Well, to be truthful, I can't keep you from doing that. I will just warn you to be mindful of the tricks of the enemy. The devil is extremely sharp, and plays on our thoughts. That's why we have to have some type of standard against which we hold every thought. That's how we combat the mental attacks of the enemy. You have to have a working knowledge of the Word and a relationship with the Father. If not, you will take cheap imitations as the real thing.

Your thoughts are important, but even in the bible, I've never seen thoughts alone change anybody's situation. They still had to get up and do. Proverbs 12:11 says, "He who tills his land will be satisfied with bread, But he who follows frivolity is devoid of understanding." We can't just dream about it, we have to work. Our thoughts are our own form of gold. Many don't see it that way, but God gave you an amazing ability to think. Even when we don't acknowledge this blessing, the devil does. That's why he attacks us with his words until they become our thoughts.

There are no mistakes in God's great plan of life.

We live in a physical body, but we are made up of a spirit and soul, which are non-physical. We live in a physical world that's built in a non-physical realm. There are no mistakes from when the grass grows, to the birth of a child. God knows you. He created you. He knows your decisions, He just needs your actions. Going back to *The Secret*, I'm not fully against its teachings. What they call "visualizing" is what the believer calls expectancy. We walk in that daily with Jesus Christ. So my question is, how many reading this book have lined their thoughts up with what God wants for them?

What if God is asking you to be a politician, but you continue to auto-suggest being an artist? Then, when things don't line up, you become mad at God. The fact is, you're not following Him. You are following what you want, because you are listening to what, or whom, you choose. The devil knows that, and gets so excited when you buy into the lies. He wants to keep a hold on your life. He wants you to believe fully in things like *The Secret*, because it brings confusion when compared to the Word of God.

The law of attraction will tell us that everything that comes into your life, you are attracting. There is some truth in that statement, but it's not completely true. The devil would like you to believe otherwise. That way, he can blame you for all the things happening in your life. He can make you hold that weight, even though Jesus told you to give it to Him. You might be at home getting abused by your spouse. Since the only thing you are attracting is a beating, you feel that there is something in you that is magnetizing his or her anger. You think it's your fault. So you hold onto the idea that if you think hard enough about your spouse changing, then it will happen. He or she will become a loving and caring husband or wife overnight. I'm not saying it could never happen, but what are the odds?

That's why we have to be in a relationship with the Lord. Two Peter 2:1-3 says, "but there were also false prophets among the people, even as there will be false teachers among you, who will secretly bring in destructive heresies, even denying the Lord who bought them, and bring on themselves swift destruction. And many will follow their destructive ways, because of whom the way of truth will be blasphemed. By covetousness they will exploit you with deceptive words; for a long time their judgment has not been idle, and their destruction does not slumber." We have to allow the Holy Spirit to show us when we are being tricked by deceptive words. This ushers in the underlying theme that you will take from the remainder of this book. We have to weather the devil's attacks, and protect our thoughts from Satan. To do that, we must first realize that our thoughts are precious.

God gave us a gift called "emotional feelings."

Our emotions tell us what our non-physical is feeling in a physical sense. Many of us live solely by our emotions. When we "feel" something, we go for it. That's not completely wrong. God does show us things through our emotions. At times, when the Holy Spirit urges us toward things, we feel it internally. God can use your emotions to guide you, but the guidance, not the emotions, is the focus.

Our emotions give us a basis to know what we need to pray for in our lives. When you are having a frustrating day, God knows that is grounds for an all-out assault from the enemy. When we "feel" frustrated, that's our emotions giving us an indication to where we need to direct our prayers. We should then pray for what's stressing us. It might be our job, the stressors of that particular morning, or another issue all together. When you feel the emotion, you have to break down the source. Most of us prefer to stay in the emotion, and let our thoughts wander. This is a critical time in our relationship with the Lord. This is when He connects with us. If a child scrapes his arm, the majority of the time, he will run to his parents. That's what God is asking us to do. He knows how our thoughts can quickly send us in an unforgiving tunnel of pain. He also knows that the right thoughts can propel us beyond any circumstances. It's just a matter of what we do when the bad thoughts, or emotions, occur.

Let's say you had several altercations with your boss. Your emotions begin to stir up, and anger begins to fill you. You acknowledge your feeling, but you don't bring it to the Lord. Instead, you try to get it under control. The devil wants you to stay at that initial level. He knows you have acknowledged the attacks, but he wants you to think the attack is over. You might not have allowed the negative treatment to make you respond, but you haven't given it to Christ. The devil might not attack you through your boss for the remainder of the day, but he will attack. He will send co-workers to upset you. He will keep you from finding things you need at your desk. He will inch-by-inch crawl up your back until it is too much. It's happens to me all the time. The reason being, I never spoke directly to my situation.

Psalm 55:22 says, "Cast your burden on the Lord, and He shall sustain you; He shall never permit the righteous to be moved." I didn't cast my cares on the Lord; I chose to fight the battle myself. Even when I thought I had won, I lost. I would try to keep my cool when bad things started to happen around me. My emotions would go back and forth throughout the day because I lacked the peace of the Lord. By the time I got off from work, I was drained. I didn't have the energy to do anything for the rest of the day. There were times when I would skip church, because I wasn't in the mood. What I really was saying was, "I am in my emotions right now." God could have had a situation lined up for me at church. God could have spoken directly to me in the sermon. Maybe I was supposed to meet someone that night for a God-given reason. That's why we have to understand the purpose of our emotions.

Negative emotions bring on a negative mood.

When you are in a negative mood, that situation tends to bring along negative thoughts. Those negative thoughts attract more negative events in your life. I'm not saying that if you don't think about negative thoughts, then your life will always be positive. I'll leave those lies to *The Secret*. Believers and non-believers should both know that life is full of peaks and valleys. There is no end-all cure for the negativity in the world.

When I was growing up, I would get so angry at people being rude and ugly to me, for no apparent reason. When I would talk about it with my mom, she would say, "Well, you know everybody isn't going to heaven. If they persecuted Jesus, how much more will they do to you, C.J.?" That was so true, and I never forgot that. Between the devil's plots, and the many people he uses as vessels, we will always be attacked until Jesus returns. Really sit with that for a moment. You have to expect that from here on out. It will make your life much easier.

Since we expect the good with the bad, we can make the transition to trusting God through it all. Now we have a foundation of hope. We know that we endure pain from the enemy, but we can't give him all the credit. Some of that negativity surrounding you was invited by you. I'm the type of person that you call if you want a solution to your problem. I don't like it when people call me just to complain on the phone. I'm not against people venting their problems to me, but if you don't want to find a solution, then you're just being negative. What type of person complains for an hour, then gets off the phone to find another person to hear their woes? Believe me, there are plenty.

When you are negative, you tend to search for others who "understand" what you are going through. When you reach an individual who speaks positivity to your situation, many of you will leave him or her to find someone that can relate through sympathy. You can't see that their sympathy can sometimes be a hindrance. Many of us don't need to hear, "Girl, that happened to you? That's terrible. I'm so sorry. It's gonna be okay." The one that you feel is being rude could be your voice of truth. God could have sent that person to build you up.

When I was in the army, everybody used to complain in the office. I, too, was included in that group. One day, I was dreading to go in the building. I sat in my car and prayed, begging God to help me. I guess I wanted God to do something to keep me from going to work. I laugh at it now, but I was so serious back then. Of course, He did no such thing. What He did do was speak to me through the Holy Spirit. He told me to change my attitude. He asked me how many times did I pray for employment, when I didn't have anything. He then asked me how many times had I gone to work with a positive mindset. He pulled my card. When I went into the building, I changed my perception of my job. This allowed me to see from the outside looking in. I noticed that all of the negative people were huddled together. They would complain all day about everything. It made the people who actually worked very upset, which brought more negativity their way. Every time a task came down, they looked for the complainers. Ever since the day I came to work with a positive attitude, doors began to open for me. My busy-work load lightened, and my real responsibilities increased. God blessed me with more meaningful tasks, and I felt better about completing them. God changed my situation because of my attitude. By me being positive, even when it became stressful, I was surrounded by more positivity. Ambitious people began to befriend me. That was very important.

Many of you have lived your entire life thinking negatively. God has given you great ideas, or shown you visions of yourself working in some awesome capacity, yet you deflect them. You have a negative mood toward life. You use that reason to self-medicate with alcohol, drugs, anger, sex, food, etc. You might feel that these things deflect the pain of your negative thoughts, but believe me, Satan is still coming. He wants to keep you stagnant around stagnant people.

I remember when I was in college. My parents have always pushed me to do well in school: they would tell me to find a seat in the front of the class, and I would do so. I pledged Alpha Phi Alpha fraternity the second semester of my freshman year. Being in a fraternity brought new friends, some of whom were in my Accounting 101 class. Normally, I sit in the front, but all of my friends sat in the back. They pleaded with me to sit with them; therefore, I did so. The entire time, I could hear my parents' voices, telling me to move up. I just ignored it. My new friends and I would talk and disrupt class. I knew that wasn't why my parents were spending all that money for me to attend college, but I couldn't resist the temptation. When I got my first test score back, it was horrendous. I scored a 63 out of 100. As I sat in devastation, I looked over to my friends. They also scored low, but seemed to be content with it. At that moment, I had to make a decision. I grabbed all of my stuff and asked the teacher if I could move. My friends complained about my departure, but I knew I had to go. Their negativity was attracting more negativity. My teacher smiled at my request. She told me later that I was too smart to be allowing others to keep me from my goals in life. She too could see the negativity, and the pitfalls of it surrounding me.

If I had stayed in that seat, I know I would have failed that class. In turn, I would have been upset at the grade, not at myself. That negative emotion could have transcended into an overall negative mood about school. Then who knows what could have happened. Maybe I would have dropped out? I don't know. All I knew was that I was surrounded by negativity, and that I had invited it by my own free will.

God is trying to block some of the things or people presently in your lives. You can't see your future, but God can. He is trying to preserve your emotions. He knows that once you go through, by your own free will, that situation is going to bring you negative emotions. He also knows that once you have those negative emotions, the enemy will work nonstop to switch those emotions into your mood. Satan will do this by attacking your thoughts at your moment of weakness. That mood will cripple your defense, allowing the enemy more access to you. That weakness might allow you to listen to and receive words that are not of God, for your life. Again, your thoughts are so important. You have to protect them at all costs.

God always has a reason for speaking warnings to us. He is all-knowing, and protects us from things to come. One Corinthians 2:9-10 says, "Eye has not seen, nor ear heard, nor have entered into the heart of man the things which God has prepared for those who love Him. But God has revealed them to us through His Spirit. For the Spirit searches all things, yes, the deep things of God." We just have to quit being prideful, and receive the truth. That truth includes being mindful of your emotions, and how they change your mood.

God granted us the ability to choose the images we want to think about and dwell upon in our minds.

Isaiah 26:3 states, "You keep him in perfect peace whose mind is stayed on you, because he trusts in you." Do you believe that? As a young boy, I didn't watch too much television. I mainly watched ESPN, movies, and music videos. Those music videos captivated me. My friends and I would watch rap artists like Tupac, living lawless. That enticed me. I wanted that lifestyle. From females dancing around half naked, to rappers cursing people out, I wanted it all. Those images became my thoughts. I would dwell on these thoughts and visions until they became my reality. Next thing I knew, I was head first in the streets, doing everything I was told not to do. I was caught up in the allure of no acknowledgement of sin. I didn't know it at the time; I thought they were living life.

As I'm getting older, God is still correcting many images I have adopted as real life. I would walk around as a young man, calling women "b***hes" as if it were their names. I thought those moments were harmless, to myself and to the females I spoke about. I didn't know that, by treating women that way, it would place a block on me. By acting out the images of the television in my mind, it personally made me lack intimacy with my wife, years later. The men I saw on television didn't show weakness. I never saw them glorifying marriage. Many men today still don't; we treat it as a punishment. That's a whole other topic that I won't touch upon.

The point is, I became what I thought about. Those things that I invited into my spirit became me. So when my wife, Jennifer, wanted to lay in bed and cuddle, I would break away. It made me feel soft. I thought that was just my normal feeling, but it wasn't. I yearned to connect with my wife; I just couldn't break through the images I was portraying at the moment. That stomach-turning feeling would come to me every time we laid down and stared deeply at each other. That feeling was the same excitement I felt the first time I laid eyes on her. I knew it was right. I just couldn't get past the words the devil would speak to me at the same moment. He would remind me that I was a tough guy. He would say, "Real men don't act this way. You're losing control, C.J."

This particular problem burdened my wife and me for years. I would pray for a change, but every time, I would respond the same way. Now that I look back, God was definitely moving on my behalf. He had to really sit me down and show me where the problem lay, before it could be resolved. I am forever thankful because it clarified some other issues attached to it. From that, and other experiences, I have become aware of the images I place before myself.

Before you get all excited and applaud my efforts, I'm not saying that I cut myself off from society. Romans 12:2, paraphrased, says do not be conformed to this world, but be transformed by the renewing of your mind. It doesn't say separate yourself from the world. If we did, who would we tell about the love of Jesus Christ? It says we are to be renewed while in this world. We are to stand out and be different. I still watch movies and listen to rap music with cursing. I also have grown to listen to jazz, alternative, metal, gospel, Christian hip-hop music, and the list goes on. I like music: it's a gift from the Creator.

Many of my brothers and sisters in Christ would look at me sideways when I told this to them. They would quote scriptures such as Ephesians 4:29, which says, "Let no corrupt word proceed out of your mouth, but what is good for necessary edification, that it may impart grace to the hearers." I would respond that they were right. When I was younger, I didn't know how words, from music or any source, could affect my spirit. I should have, though, because I used it to change my mood. When I would get upset, I never ran to my bible. I never got on my knees and prayed to my Father. I would close my door and go to the church of Jay-Z. I would just let HOV (Jay-Z) play for hours, teaching me about life: or so I thought. His words changed my thoughts, which ultimately changed me.

Now I am conscious of the negativity that surrounds certain songs and lyrics, but I can't say that it's all bad. Even if the song has cursing and an overall derogatory message, there still can be some good within it. I think about my uncle, who has a very slick mouth. He curses and says some off the wall things. I mean, REALLY OFF THE WALL. So should I never listen to him when he gives me advice? Absolutely not. It's my responsibility to sift through the nonsense, and look for the gold nuggets. Out of a ten minute BS conversation, he might say something that could change my life for the better. It's on me to trust the Holy Spirit.

If you are reading this and saying, "That is totally not the Word of God," then riddle me this: should I shun them because of what they say? If you say yes, then should I shun you, not if, but when, you say or do something contrary to the Word of God? Should your kids or family members quit listening to school teachers if they don't believe in God? I'm not condoning the negative examples in rap, or in any type of art. In the end though, art is art and people are people. Art is expression. It's not their job to make better music. It's our job to teach our kids to make conscious decisions about life. They will do what they will to do.

You can't expect the world to change. We can only allow God to work on our behalf to change us. That change starts with the images we place before us, and the thoughts that accompany those images. One day I might be able to only listen to gospel music, but I can't say I am there today. I would tell my church friends that when I was going through trials, many times, songs from rappers like T.I. or Jay-Z got me through them. Now that I'm older, I know it was the hand of Jesus. Still, I can't lie and say that I didn't learn things from these people. God knew that. He can use anything or anyone He chooses to get through to His children. I just had to learn what to look for while digging through the trash.

I say all this to say, we have to be mindful of what we place before ourselves, especially during our moments of vulnerability. Also, when it comes to images, we have to be conscious of what we think is a "good image" from God. I've seen everything from posts on Facebook to stories on CNN that flash images and words before our faces. We will send hate messages to gay people because the visual of God hating gays was placed before us by man. My people (African-Americans) will continue to digress because of the low images we place on ourselves. Many of you reading this will mistreat someone today solely based upon a prejudice that was presented to you years ago.

We work off of the images we see. That's why it was written in Proverbs 4:20-23, "My son, give attention to my words; Incline your ear to my sayings. Do not let them depart from your eyes; Keep them in the midst of your heart; For they are life to those who find them, And health to all their flesh. Keep your heart with all diligence, For out of it spring the issues of life." God's Words paint images for us. They allow us to see others, ourselves, and our situations from the proper perspective. God tells us to keep our hearts diligent, because from it springs the issues of life. Those issues are the same issues God is addressing for you, while you read this book. He wants you to make sure that you have the proper images in your eyesight, so that everything else aligns with your new vision. With a proper image placed on your mind, anything is possible.

Many have a hard time realizing that our thoughts bring action.

Those actions, though they come from little ole you, can affect the world. Whether you take from somebody else's thoughts or come up with your own, you can turn those thoughts into ideas and those ideas into actions. When you wake up, what's the first thing you think about? You may not know it, but that "thing" you focus on is what fuels your day. This thought can range from bills that are past due to just being thankful for your loving family. You can also wake up and instantly check your Facebook account, which translates into being social or possibly the idea of one day being accepted by the "in" crowd of people you associate with daily. I want you to really think about what drives you throughout the day.

For myself, I had to realize that my day was surrounded by my early morning thoughts of being a failure. The fear of not being adequate ran me ragged for the remainder of the day. Even though this fear often forced me to get off my butt and do something, I would still deviate from my initial plans I set for my life. Without noticing, I would tend to drift from my goals and end up in some uncharted area. "Why does this continue to happen to me?" I would ask God. His reply was that I needed to take control of my thoughts. Due to me not having a solid roadmap, built around the faith and focus of God's promises for me in my life, I was depending on my own strength. Being mortal, I was only created to handle so much. When the going got tough, out of fear of losing, I would put my head down and charge full speed to my destination. Thinking I was winning because of "my" efforts alone, I would look up, only to realize that by keeping my head down toward the pavement, I had lost sight of my goal. My aggressive efforts did allow me to gain something, just not the something that I had initially set out to get.

28

Let me give you an example so that you can relate it to your current situation. When I graduated college, I had this thought pattern that the world was about to open up the floodgates to me. In my mind, NOBODY would be able to stop me from climbing the ladder of success. I mapped out my career goals, and one-by-one I started to ascend Mount Go Get It. When I got into the working world, various variables began to take form that I wasn't prepared to conquer at the time. I was immediately bombarded with negative thoughts from family and friends about every decision I was making in regards to my career progression. Those thoughts had an effect. Next, I was surrounded by colleagues who rejected the "team" ideology, and instead made it known that we were in competition. This made me feel isolated. When all of my emotions and thoughts began to boil over, I made a decision. I decided to put my head down and push through all obstacles, never looking up until I got where I wanted to go. Now this wasn't a bad decision, but my thoughts were not guided by God's plan for me. I did pray, but I felt that God wasn't moving as fast as I could. Plus, deep down at the time, I didn't truly believe that God would control my every step. Even though I read throughout my lifetime that God wants me to surrender my will to His and just walk with Him, I just couldn't exercise faith on that level. My mindset was asking questions like, "What if He isn't real?" "If He is real, does He really want me to depend on Him for everything or just some things?" "I only have so many years on this earth, and I refuse to lose some following this myth of full dependency on God." I just couldn't connect that all I had to do was commune with God, listen to direction from the Holy Spirit, and do EXACTLY what God tells me to do at that given moment. So I did what anybody would do: I went to go get what was due to me.

The moment I put my head down, I lost my sense of direction and connection with the Lord. Then little nuances began to pull me off this track I had created. If I were at a job that God gave me, I would leave it because someone there made me upset. The devil used them to push me out of my blessing. Now, if I had had my eyes and ears focused on God's plan for me, I may have stayed and endured to receive the lesson needed to go to the next part of His plan for me. Instead, God had to place me under a new employer and restart my process. I felt I was in control of my destiny, but in the end I was only running full speed in circles. I was a dog chasing his tail. I got enjoyment out of the process. I felt like I achieved something because of the amount of unrelenting effort I was placing in my daily tasks. In the end, like a dog, I was right where I had started. Soak that in.

Think over the years how much of yourself you have put into something with your head down, telling yourself, "I am determined to make it through and reach my goals." After you finally quit moving and assess your progress, you realize that you are right where you started. Maybe small things have changed, but ultimately, that situation has remained the same. Then, ask yourself, "how many times did the Holy Spirit give me direction and I denounced those thoughts and impulses?" Some of us don't even really inquire of the Lord and His direction for our lives. We just make decision after decision, and then call out to God once we dig a ditch too deep. All of your circumstances in your life stem from one single solitary thought. That one thought is then followed by other thoughts, essentially bringing you to make actions based upon those thoughts. That is our process.

Now that we have acknowledged this, let's use it to our advantage. First, let's submit our plans to God's plan for us. If you skip over this step, it will come back to bite you later. God owns and is in control of everything in this world. Even if you think you have achieved something great in your life by your own effort, I promise you God made that happen for you. You just didn't give Him the credit. So if you do become a millionaire, do you think God cares about the money or having a relationship with you? He can take that money just as quick as He loaned it to you. He will make sure you know that He is the one blessing you, because He wants you to pay true homage. Just quickly saying thank you and then running to go play with your newly acquired toys is a no-go. He wants to bless you. He also wants you to commune with Him.

Now that we have set the foundation, let's do our part and let God do the rest. He will show up, I promise. Just have faith and believe. Once we submit to the Creator, let's use one of the gifts that he gave us. This gift is called imagination. God gave us the ability to see ourselves in the future, beyond our present circumstances. Through that imagination, I can create mental pictures. I can see myself in beautiful relationships, successful, money coming in, etc. I dictate what I see. If you want greater wealth, visualize it coming into your life. I mean visualize it so strongly that it feels as if it is already here.

Free will allows us to think what we want, and that thinking process can put us in either a positive or a negative mindset. This mindset will draw either more negative or more positive experiences. No one can cause you to think about something you don't want to think about. That's powerful. Often times, we blame our negative actions on others because of the things that are happening in our lives. Those things are external factors that have an outward effect on us. I know we have to acknowledge any issues that arise in our lives. I get it. What I am saying is that if I let the thoughts of the problem linger to long, I won't make it to the solution side. Many times we think we are conjuring up a solution, but instead we are just running after our tails. You sit and stress for an entire day, only to realize that you still haven't come up with a solid plan to execute a solution. Then when we come up with a solution (e.g., someone in a financial hardship situation decides to sell dope to fix his or her problem), most often these decisions aren't beneficial for us long term. Many times, they only cure our short-term problems.

This goes back to the point me made earlier: even before we decide what our thoughts will be on the situation, we need to seek God's face. That way when we begin to think, not about the stressful problem but more about a positive solution, it will be in line with God's will and plan for our lives. All of this is inter-connected. This way, we focus on Christ and not on our problem. We seek solutions, but desire a relationship and proper guidance from the Lord over what we are praying to gain from the relationship. That's how you get the right thoughts to gain momentum in your pursuit of a great life within the world God gave us dominion over. Remember that all great leaders, from Christians to non-believers, have one thing in common: we become what we think of ourselves.

Now ask yourself, "What Do I Really Want?" Do you want wealth, a great marital relationship, good health, prosperity, a great business? God is the architect of your life, and YOU are the architect of your thoughts. At any time, you can tap into this infinite resource of positive thoughts. There is an abundance of people within this magnificent world that seem to have positivity overflowing within them. Attach yourself to those people. Ask God to send you people to help change your mindset.

Be cautioned that before God answers your prayer, He will work on you internally. You can't ask God for an outward blessing without expecting Him to ask you to change inwardly. You have to think, most positive people are positive because they limit the amount of negative people they associate with throughout the day. So God isn't going to place you under these types of people until you are at a certain point within yourself. That's because your negativity can be detrimental to their mindset if they aren't strong enough to pull you to their side. You can never attract into your life something that is not already in harmony with you. We live in an orderly and precise universe where energy attracts energy. Negative thoughts produce negative energy, essentially attracting negative people. Negative people then speak negative words, which brings you back to the first phase of having negative thoughts. It is a deadly perpetual cycle. Understand that the "good" you want in this life is already here. All you have to do is get in harmony with it. You do that with your own thinking, and substituting the will of God for your will.

Our belief systems stem from how we evaluate something.

The more we evaluate something, the stronger our beliefs get, good or bad. The way you think about something, that's the direction that the situation will go. Our thoughts have frequency and energy. You send off that energy every time you think and speak out your negative or positive thoughts. Again, think about the people with whom you currently associate. Analyze them. Who's successful and who isn't? That success can even be from a negative action. Their actions are not the focus right now. Just analyze their mindsets. What do these individuals say when they speak about their beliefs? Are they go-getters? Are they negative, speaking down on themselves? Do they seek the approval of others? Do they shy away from possible pain and failure? If they are successful, what do they do when they hit an obstacle? Do they plan? Do they learn from their mistakes? The reason I ask these questions is because a mindset is a mindset. If you can sell drugs, which is illegal, and be successful, you can sell real estate, which is legal, and be successful. The mindset doesn't change, just the product. On the flip side, if you can't even handle the pressure of your part-time job without speaking death on yourself, why would anybody dive into a relationship with you and give you his or her all? All you would do is bring that person to the dark side.

When we speak about individuals like Joseph Stalin or Adolf Hitler, the first thing that people speak about is their actions. True, their actions were horrific, but think about how strong their thoughts had to be to commit to something of that magnitude. That means they took control of their thoughts, just for the wrong purpose. Nevertheless, there is much to be learned from these men. They had that mental spark. The same mental spark you have when you awake in the morning; the same mental spark you get when you realize your motives for what you are doing. These men knew why they were trying to dominate the world. You can knock their ill will toward God and His plan for creation, but you can't knock their mental capacity to make their thoughts streamline them to their desired results.

So let's change our thoughts, our words, and our actions. You speak what you think about most, and you attract what you speak about most of all. The stronger our belief, the more we speak about the things we believe in. That can be positive, like believing that you can achieve greatness; or it can be negative, like believing that you aren't worthy of being successful in anything. Even when you dwell on things you don't want, that's still negative energy. For example, constantly focusing on the fact that you "don't want to fail" still hinders you from going full speed toward your goal. You'll pace yourself, forever looking back to see if failure has caught up to you. We should be running with God full steam ahead to that destination we imagined for ourselves.

So focus on the things you do want and keep that focus. If not, that focus will still be present but just allocated toward something else. We should be making conscious efforts to take control of our thoughts. Put on some music, sing, think of something beautiful. Whatever you decide to think about, make sure it is positive and keep those thoughts centered in your mind. For some, they can focus solely on God. For others, they can't just eat the Word of God and be fed. Some need external triggers like their family, or the idea of success: that's okay. Praise God that He is greater and sovereign compared to us humans who occupy this land. He has an innate power which allows Him to use whoever and whatever to redirect your attention on Him and His plans for your life, which includes His desire for you to walk with Him.

God blesses our efforts because of the covenant He made with His people. We follow His covenant requirements and live by His kingdom principles because we love Him. His rules govern our hearts because we ultimately know, as believers, that they are in place for our good. God wouldn't require me to stay monogamous with my wife unless adultery brought something with it that could harm me. If I sleep around, I can potentially bring diseases back to my spouse or impregnate another woman. God didn't plan for me to step out and start another family; he already blessed me with what I need. Therefore, under free will, this would mean that I made a decision that showed I didn't need God and His direction for my life. Essentially, I'm telling God, "I got it."

When we have these types of disconnect with the Father, then He can't help us when we are attacked by the enemy. Going back to the analogy stated earlier, you will finally lift up your bowed head and realize that you aren't where you were supposed to be in life. So again I will reiterate with authority, "YOU ARE WHERE YOU ARE IN YOUR LIFE BECAUSE OF THE DECISIONS YOU HAVE MADE, AND THOSE DECISIONS CAME FROM YOUR THOUGHTS!" We guard our thoughts because Satan knows if he can gain access to our thoughts, he will be in control of our actions. If Satan controls our actions…then he controls US!

Part III

WAR

<hr/>

The devil sets us up.

The devil tells us lies about what we can and cannot do. If he controls our thoughts, he can control our bodies and our actions. "So how does this relate to being in a war?" one might ask. Let's get a visual representation. I was enlisted in the United States Army for six years. Even though I grew up as a military brat, due to both my mother and father being in the army, my personal experience was a hard one to wrap my brain around. I came up in a Godly and very positive home. My parents had rules, but for the most part I was free to roam as I pleased. I cherished that freedom, and pushed its boundaries daily. Their absence of jurisdiction or abundance of trust, depending on how you view it, allowed me to get heavy in the streets. It were as if carefree Willy Wonka got placed in a jail cell with Rick James. My innocent chocolate was replaced with weed rolled by women whose thighs matched the size of the blunt—THICK! In this environment, I felt even more alive. Nobody was around to tell us what we were doing was right or wrong. We were walking proudly to the beat of our own drums.

So fast forward years later to me in army fatigues getting yelled at by some random guy that claims he outranks me, and based on that principle alone, I should listen and follow every direction out his mouth. Now if I didn't know what it felt like to be free, I would have probably conformed to this mindset instantly. I would look about and see other soldiers running around with their heads cut off trying to please these superiors at any cost. They would even mistreat each other just to get the approval of their leadership. It disturbed me that nobody would question these commands given to them, no matter how outrageous they were in theory. Then one day God showed me the reason. The Army as a culture was in control of their thoughts.

Even when some of my colleagues would get off work, they would still think like they were at work. Some would come home and run their families like it was an extension of their workplace, barking orders and demanding respect from a militant perspective. Others would be so nervous that they might miss a call from their supervisor that they stayed constantly on alert. All this places your mind in a state to where your physical actions manifest your thoughts. Now look at me during that time. Because of how I grew up, my mindset was, "Once I leave the office, I'm off work. Don't call my phone because I promise you I'm not going to answer." I would literally tell that to my boss. So when I got home, I was still me.

The Army never fully broke me because my mind was too strong. I praise God for that. Still, the military felt that strategy of thought control was necessary because they deployed numerous soldiers to hostile environments where the casualties were countless. They needed to have dominion over our thoughts, so they could contain the group and move forward to complete the mission. To them, survival is the big picture, so having control over our thoughts was a necessary evil. If any military member is reading this and says they don't agree, just think back to your basic training days. Before they taught us one thing, the drill sergeants made sure they had our attention and controlled our thoughts through scare tactics. They knew if they were successful, the body would line up and we would follow them regardless of what was asked of us. So all of this has been said to bring acknowledgement to the reader that mind control is a real and valid thing. From football coaches to pimps, the same principle still applies; if I can control your thoughts, your actions will soon follow.

Let's now go over to a biblical application. In Genesis, God creates Adam and Eve. He allows them the freedom to rule on earth and only gives them one law, which is to not eat from the Tree of Life. He didn't use mind control tactics on them, nor does He on us today. On the contrary, He gave them a gift called free will that allowed them to decide freely on any given issue. Then Satan comes in the likeness of a serpent and persuades Eve to eat the apple from the forbidden tree. In Genesis 3:4-5, the serpent tells Eve, "You will not surely die. For God knows that in the day you eat of it your eyes will be opened, and you will be like God, knowing good and evil." Satan lied to Eve to control her thoughts. He didn't control them in a supernatural way of making her do something outside her will, yet he produced curiosity to a degree that made her contemplate it until her thoughts were manifested through her actions. Essentially the serpent called God a liar. He dominated her mind with thoughts that her fair God was withholding valuable knowledge from her and Adam. Satan attacked Eve's pride.

Now take a step back and view this entire transaction with an objective perspective. Satan didn't just say some generalized negative comments about God. He also didn't turn into a big beastly creature and force the apple down Eve's throat to make her sin. He would not have spoken such direct statements of deceit against God to Eve unless he had a very specific motive. He used a war tactic. He knew if he had her attention, it would be possible to capture her thoughts; then, if he captured her thoughts, her actions would soon align and SHE would commit the sin. This seems like a propaganda war tactic to me. Satan was head-hunting with this one.

Never forget that we are always in battle with the enemy.

Ephesians 6:10-12 says, "Finally, my brethren, be strong in the Lord and in the power of His might. Put on the whole armor of God, that you may be able to stand against the wiles of the devil. For we do not wrestle against flesh and blood, but against principalities, against powers, against the rulers of the darkness of this age, against spiritual hosts of wickedness in the heavenly places." Just because you are ignorant to Satan's plan of destruction for God's creation, or outright deny his existence, doesn't mean there isn't a plan or that he doesn't exist.

When I deployed to Iraq, I was given missions outside the wire in the heart of the war. Along with our mission-oriented tasks, I also had a personal task called staying alive. Beyond the scope of these two groupings, I couldn't tell you why we were there. I could say we were fighting for freedom, or because of the events that happened on September 11, but even then that wasn't the full reason I was there. That wasn't the full reason any of us were there. Up top in the White House, I'm sure the president and his men had an agenda for placing us in that hostile environment. Their motive could have been a selfless act of love and protection toward the Iraqi people. It could have also been a selfish desire to financially fill their pockets at the expense of various brave men and women surrendered to the hands of death. A small sacrifice for the greater good in their eyes. To be totally honest we will never know; but the point to be made is that us not knowing the motive doesn't mean that there isn't a motive for the war. The devil surely has a plan he is executing daily on God's people, and the term "God's people" isn't just defined by believers. God made everybody in His image, even the individuals who deny His existence. He provides for us all, and forewarns us alike by giving us insight on Satan's plans through the scriptures.

You have to expect the attacks; it would be a deadly mistake to think otherwise. One Peter 5:8 states, "Be sober, be vigilant; because your adversary the devil walks about like a roaring lion, seeking whom he may devour." He kills our kids and destroys our lives with things like hate, greed, envy, adultery, etc. He takes all of God's wonderful gifts, including people, and uses them for his evil. He carefully plots against us, being patient and methodical in his plans of attack. No matter how he chooses to implement his plans, the end result remains constant. He will work to control your thoughts and make you respond in your actions to carry out his Godless will for your life.

If you look back at a typical day in your life, tell me what you see. If you got upset at your kids in the morning because you were rushing and they were moving slow, did their non-responsiveness or your thoughts make you snap on them? You look at them and say to yourself, "Didn't I tell them to get ready for school ten minutes ago?" Then you hear an answer to your voice continue the conversation, saying, "Yep, you did tell them that. They don't listen to you at all. You have no control. Are you gonna let it go down like this?" Next thing you know, you are infuriated. You lash out at them, verbally abusing them or worse, you physically beat the hell out of them and then verbally abuse them. Now I'm not saying don't chastise your children. I have had more than my share of beatings growing up. They were needed, to be totally honest, because I was unruly at times. I'm just saying there has to be some patience and love in the reprimand because chastisement is for correction with a lesson attached at the end. It is not for you, as the parent, a way to release your frustration at the present moment. After you have beat your child like Joe Jackson and they are all balled up in a corner crying, you have that reflection moment and realize, "I did just kind of go off the deep end a little." That leap into the tender area between child scolding and child abuse was fueled by the enemy using the same war tactic that he used since the first sin with Eve. He spoke to you in your mind to make you act out your thoughts of frustration and inferiority in the physical. Your kids might have needed that beating, but not the extra intensity you added that derived from your "I will regain my power and respect" complex. Again, he's cunning in his approach.

To combat darts from the enemy, we have to be concerned with what's acceptable to God.

Most of the time, we can't control our actions because we can't control our thoughts. He wages war on the mind because a stronghold on the mind, which is non-physical, will bring forth negative actions that will affect the world in a physical sense. For example, my mom loved listening to Whitney Houston sing when I was growing up. She also became very fond of her acting, gazing big-eyed at the television screen while Whitney amazed us in such films as *The Bodyguard*, *Waiting to Exhale* and *The Preacher's Wife*. It wasn't that she was a fanatic, but Whitney's voice and ability to be open and free translated into a sense of strength for my mom. By watching Whitney sing, she somehow gained and understood a piece of herself. Whitney would never know what she gave my mom; she never knew my mom. Still, God's plan of love allowed my mother to be blessed by something He placed in another individual. Of course we all know the end to the story. Whitney got caught up in drugs with Bobby Brown and ultimately they became her downfall. She was found dead in a bathtub at the Beverly Hilton Hotel. Her death affected my mother's spirit for a while. With all the talent God had blessed Whitney, and the success that followed her, my mom just couldn't grasp why she would throw it all away. I know that comment might seem one-sided because life is more than tangible success, but because I know my mother, that statement really meant, "She motivated me with her drive and soothed me with her voice. I hate that the devil took another wonderful person off this earth."

Death is such a common thing on this earth that sometimes we tend to overlook the circumstances surrounding it. We all know we have to die. The day that beautiful daughter of yours is born, her death timer starts to tick. We are born to die. When you look a little closer though, some deaths are before their time, and we all know it. When you can look at the news and see a teen like Trayvon Martin losing his life at such an early age, all minds connect throughout the world in one accord thinking, "That's a life that was taken way too early." Satan knows what he is doing. To us in the physical realm, that's just another person that lost his life. To Satan in the spiritual realm, he's thinking, "Not only did I just kill off that one person; I just killed off everybody's blessing that was attached to that person." Think about it in this way. What if Trayvon Martin had grown up and became a basketball coach? He would have been in a position to sow seeds of ambition and love into numerous kids' lives every year. Instead of being in the streets, those kids might have stayed positive due to his mentorship. You never know, one of those kids he might have coached could have become the next LeBron James, Michael Jordan, Barak Obama, etc.

Again, if the reader thinks that point is far-fetched, reflect back on your own life. How many great accomplishments in your life have you already achieved because another person spoke words of encouragement to you? How many pitfalls have you avoided because God blessed you with the right person at the right time to help you through? Now let's flip the coin. To how many situations have you responded negatively because of someone talking down to you, making you feel some type of way? Proverbs 18:21 says, "Death and life are in the power of the tongue, and those who love it will eat its fruit." The enemy knows that if everyone on planet Earth followed the teachings of Jesus Christ and started to speak life to one another that the world would change instantly and drastically for the better. Walls such as racism and the perpetual gap between social classes would be eradicated. He knows that he really doesn't have any power to make you do something because of free will. The only tactic he has is to prompt you by your thoughts. Satan will make you fearful even though 2 Timothy 1:7 says, "For God has not given us a spirit of fear, but of power and of love and of a sound mind." How many people do you know, including yourself, that are so scared to enjoy life? We are scared of people, rejection, failure, success, being broke, being rich, dying, living, so on and so forth. Ask yourself, "why?"

When I was younger, I was a chubby child. It was that time in my life where I really started to be attracted to females. I was very enthusiastic about my approach and my intentions were honest. If I told a girl she was pretty, I meant it. There wasn't a side motive. Even though I was pure in purpose, I was also oblivious, thinking these same females I were approaching were also genuine in their actions toward me. On the contrary, I was introduced to my chubbiness. They would tell me I was cute but I was too fat to date. They all could have been sports agents because they did not budge on their negotiation at all. I was labeled the cool fat friend. This negative logo seemed as though it was stamped on my forehead and trademarked me throughout the school. It massacred my confidence. I became fearful about the thing that made me who I was. I quit being an extrovert and kept to myself. The silver lining to the story is because I was everybody's chubby friend, I became popular. Over time I lost all that weight and you know those females came running back like they were training for the Olympics. I can't lie though.

I was still fearful to be that nice, decent guy I once was. The devil had a hold of my thoughts, which translated into a fear from nothing really. He created it and I held onto it like a child with a teddy bear when the lights go out. I made it bigger than life, when in fact it was just that...life.

Now that I'm thirty-one years old, I have been around people long enough to know that I will always have someone tell me something hurtful or derogatory. That's that power of life and death we spoke about earlier. If I let it hit me and I hold onto it, those words aren't just words anymore. They become my thoughts. As I focus on the thoughts, I react to either the thought or the way the thought makes me feel in the physical (e.g., depressed, anxious, excited, etc.), and that action I chose becomes life or death to me.

The Merriam-Webster dictionary defines the word "think" as, "to believe that something is true, that a particular situation exists, that something will happen, etc." It is a present tense verb, or better said, a present tense action. To think is a form of preparation. You are forming something in your mind right now. The Merriam-Webster dictionary defines the word "thought" as, "an idea, plan, opinion, picture, etc., that is formed in your mind." Something that you think of. It is a noun, which in school they teach names a person, place, thing, or idea. A thought is a plan of action. Unlike the verb "think" where you are still conceptualizing, "thought" means you have a clear picture. Whatever you were thinking has become real to you.

God knows His people and he has been trying to help us since day one. Philippians 4:8 says, "Finally, brethren, whatever things are true, whatever things are noble, whatever things are just, whatever things are pure, whatever things are lovely, whatever things are of good report, if there is any virtue and if there is anything praiseworthy, meditate on these things." He is telling us to not just go through life aimlessly while we react to whatever our minds can conjure up. You will be signing a spiritual death certificate. He's preparing you for the war because it has always been about the minds of God's creation.

Satan can't handle positive thoughts.

He is stopped in his tracks. What he meant for bad, God can turn into good. Hold on for dear life. Take Joseph for example. He was sold into slavery by his own brothers. Put yourself in his shoes. You could be thinking at this point, "I can't believe my own flesh and blood set me up to die. I will get my revenge if I ever get out of this situation." You could also be thinking, "God, how could you let this happen to me?" "I didn't deserve this. YOU'RE NOT REAL!" Ironically, if you read the entire story, God's hands were definitely guiding this bad situation.

A point needs to be made here though. The brothers had free will to decide how to treat their brother. Satan spoke to their hearts and they received his words. They acted out those feelings by selling Joseph and lying about it to their father. Both actions were deceitful and void of God, but both actions were their own doing. Going back to Joseph, his brothers probably thought he would be sold as a common laborer completing extensive construction projects in very harsh conditions. Working under those conditions will make any young man's lifespan short. The Lord instead showed Joseph mercy, exalting him amongst the high society Egyptians from a slave to a ruler. He began his life in Egypt as a slave for Potiphar, the captain of the palace guard.

Now I'm sure the devil was up in Joseph's head, telling him lies like, "You are going to die here in a foreign land," or, "You should be depressed. Don't you miss your family?" "Just kill yourself and get it over with; you will NEVER see your family again, Joseph!" Instead of heeding the voice of the enemy, Joseph makes the best out of a bad situation. He works extremely hard for Potiphar and in return, Potiphar puts him in charge of all of his household affairs. Genesis 39:3 says, "And his master saw that the Lord was with him and that the Lord made all he did to prosper in his hand." Potiphar couldn't have seen the spiritual covering that God had over Joseph unless it was real. Joseph had to have been speaking the Word of God boldly to himself in faith for another man to notice. He was in control of his thoughts because he knew WHO was in control of his present situation, regardless of how bleak the outcome looked.

So think, Joseph finally sees some type of light at the end of this dreary tunnel. As he sits proudly in this well-known Egyptian's home, thanking God for blessing him through the storm, he doesn't know that the devil is still plotting attacks against him. He wants to kill off Joseph, and since he seems to have a hold on his own thoughts and faith in the Lord, Satan has to use everything and everyone around him. The enemy specifically speaks to the desires of Potiphar's wife, and she begins to sexually harass Joseph. God didn't take this situation away, because she too had free will. Joseph keeps his Godly stance in the situation and denies her; therefore, she screams "rape" because she's petty. So again put yourself in Joseph's shoes. Could you see yourself crying out to God, "Am I cursed, God?" "Why can't I get a break?" "You don't love me at all. If you did, none of this stuff would be happening to me." "I didn't do anything wrong AGAIN! If I had a gun right now, I would kill myself."

God still moved on behalf of Joseph. The law in Egypt at that time allowed the slave owners to execute their slaves if they perceived them to be violent. Instead of death, Potiphar just sent Joseph to jail. Honestly, jail was a blessing to Joseph, and an example of God's favor on his life. Potiphar sent him to the royal prison, a place for the king's personal prisoners where he had command authority. Even in that prison, Joseph experienced God's loyal love. The Lord always keeps his promises by staying with His people, even in rough situations.

Genesis 39:21 states, "But the Lord was with Joseph and showed him mercy, and He gave him favor in the sight of the keeper of the prison." The keeper of the prison, who was the warden under Potiphar, committed to Joseph's hand ALL of the prisoners who were in the prison. This was to include the chief baker and the chief cupbearer of the king. They were both under arrest, awaiting the disposition of the charges against them. As a trustee of the prison, Joseph's job was to serve the high officials while they waited for their judgment. Without even knowing that these two individuals would be incarcerated, Joseph was already in a place to serve them and carry out God's plan for his life. By being in his position of authority that God granted through His favor, he is able to interpret the dreams of both the king's servants. Joseph correctly predicts, through the dream interpretation, what will happen to both men in the near future. The chief baker is executed and the chief cupbearer gets his employment status back in the king's court. Before the chief cupbearer is reinstated, Joseph asks the chief cupbearer to remember him and mention him to Pharaoh so that his case of false imprisonment could be reviewed. He probably figured since the chief cupbearer was badly treated and unfairly charged by Pharaoh, he himself would recognize the unfairness of Joseph's circumstances, beginning when he was sold into slavery, for just interpreting his own dream.

So picture Joseph, still stuck in that prison trying to hold onto his faith in a God that can't be seen with the natural eye. He doesn't know if the chief cupbearer will hold true and speak his name to Pharaoh. All Joseph can do is think...ALL DAY! He has an opportunity, but no way to check and see if it's even moving forward. Anybody reading this who has been locked up knows that feeling. It's rough on the mind when you can't get your phone call and you don't know if anybody is doing anything to get you out. It can drive you crazy, seriously. To add insult to injury, the chief cupbearer flaked on him. He didn't even speak up for Joseph. How many times have you done something nice for someone and they treated you poorly in return? This is a side note lesson for you and me. Joseph still kept the faith, knowing that God was with him. His constant string of bad circumstances didn't deter his beliefs. He had a very good grip on his thoughts because he knew the source of his strength and the great architect of his life.

Joseph was left in that prison for two years until God orchestrated his rise from a dungeon to the Egyptian throne room. I know some might ask, "Why did Joseph have to wait two whole years before God took him out his situation?" We will never know that answer in its full extent. For Isaiah 55:8-9 reads, "'For My thoughts are not your thoughts, nor are your ways My ways,' says the Lord. 'For as the heavens are higher than the earth, so are My ways higher than your ways, and My thoughts higher than your thoughts.'" The point you need to take and reflect upon for your own life is that the Lord never left Joseph. He stayed true to His promise that He would never leave nor forsake him, nor you and me. To go a little further into the verses from Isaiah chapter 55, verses 10 and 11 speak, "For as the rain comes down, and the snow from heaven, and do not return there, but water the earth, and make it bring forth and bud, that it may give seed to the sower and bread to the eater, so shall My word be that goes forth from My mouth; It shall not return to Me void. But it shall accomplish what I please, and shall prosper *in the thing* for which I sent it." "In the thing" is the key phrase. That's your circumstance that you're in RIGHT NOW!

While Joseph is still in that cell waiting on an answer from God, Pharaoh has a dream he can't interpret. The chief cupbearer then remembers Joseph and recommends him to interpret the dream for him. When Joseph comes to Pharaoh, he says to Joseph, "I have heard it said of you that you can understand a dream to interpret it." Joseph replies, "It is not me, God will give Pharaoh an answer of peace." How big is that! He could have taken all the credit at that moment. Most would say he deserved that right. God had left him in a jail cell for years, along with all the other obstacles he had to endure. This could have been his chance to make something happen on his own, telling God, "You haven't done anything for me. This is my time to provide for myself." His declaration of his belief in the true God was a bold statement to be made in the pagan courts of Pharaoh. He did not take credit for his ability to interpret dreams or use his innocence to plead for his freedom. For all he knew, he could have interpreted the dream and got sent right back to the jail. Led by the Spirit of God, Joseph revealed the meaning of the dream to him.

To summarize the dream, Joseph told Pharaoh that there would be a seven year period of great prosperity throughout the land of Egypt. Afterward, there would be another seven year period of famine so great that all the prosperity of Egypt would be forgotten. It would destroy the land. Now remember earlier when you read verses 8 and 9 of Isaiah about how our thoughts are not God's thoughts? God put Joseph in Egypt during this critical time so that He could bless Egypt through a Hebrew. Then the true and living God's blessing would become known throughout the land. God promised to bless all nations through the people of Israel. Though the Egyptians don't believe in the Lord, they are still God's people because He created them. He still cares for them and through His obligation of unconditional love, He wants to show them his grace and mercy, hoping they will turn their faces to Him.

Before we move forward, bring this to your level. How many of you know that God urges others in their spirit to pray for you daily? You might wake up and have a really blessed day. You feel upbeat for some reason, everything is falling in line, you get promoted, have a great dinner with your family, etc. You might look up to God and say thank you, not knowing that He blessed you due to another individual being unselfish in his or her prayers. The next day you go to work and your boss is a jerk. He is Saddam Hussein in the flesh and you can't handle it. You pray for help and you hear a soft voice say, "Just pray for him right now." You disregard the voice because you are so pissed at him, you dare not speak a blessing into his life. Ask yourself this question though: who's praying for him? He might go home to a family that doesn't even believe in Christ. He doesn't know that the devil is using him because he doesn't believe in Satan. He's an easy vessel to be used by the enemy. It's really not his fault, to be totally honest. God places His people in certain situations, regardless of how uncomfortable they are, so that you can be a blessing and an instrument of his glory. How can the non-believers see God move if they never acknowledge His existence? God needs to use us so they can hear what the Holy Spirit places in us to speak, and see the manifestation of His power.

By us staying true to the Word of God, through good and bad times, we will be a light to the lost and give them a true reference to the power of God. Pharaoh not only believes Joseph's dream interpretation; He also believes that God has given Joseph a special gift of wisdom and insight. He puts him in charge of gaining and managing the grain supply that will be distributed to all the nations during this horrific famine. God fought these uphill battles for Joseph. All he had to do was remain faithful through the hard times and operate his gift when given the opportunity. There is more to Joseph's story, but in the end, not only was he able to provide for the nations during the famine, but he was also able to provide for the same family that sold him off. God allowed Joseph to be reunited with his loved ones. He tells his brothers in Genesis 45:5, "But now, do not therefore be grieved or angry with yourselves because you sold me here; for God sent me before you to preserve life." WOW! With all that heartache he went through, he still had the peace of mind to understand that it was all part of God's plan. With the king's blessing, Joseph was able to invite his entire family to move down to northern Egypt for the remaining five years of the famine. He didn't even hold out on them out of anger. He instead used his situation as a blessing to them.

The only way he could be free from the hatred is to understand that he was in control of his thoughts. He might have been down at times; he's human. The fact still remains, he kept the faith and did right in the eyesight of God. He never let the words of the enemy make him turn his back on his Lord and Savior. So when you are going through trials, just think about what God did for Joseph and his family. Jeremiah 29:11 says, "For I know the thoughts that I think toward you, says the Lord, thoughts of peace and not of evil, to give you a future and a hope." God is so amazing.

So the next question for you is: how badly do you want your freedom?

Are you prepared to fight? Do you really want to know the truth or are you content with just playing church? This war is real. The spiritual body count over the course of our human existence is mind-blowing. So many people are searching for an obvious solution to how to deal with the calamities of this world, yet continue to deny the truth when it is placed before them. We allow various things, big or small, to take our joy so quickly. I just feel we look at the right things from the wrong perspective.

If I grew up wanting to play basketball, I have to understand the rules of the game. How odd would it be to write a letter to the NBA commissioner saying, "I don't understand why I have to dribble up and down the court. I feel it would be more effective for us to be able to place the ball on the ground and kick it instead of dribbling." He would probably respond, "Mr. Reed, I appreciate your concerns, but these rules of the game have been in place way before you and I were even conceived. If you still feel this way, your best bet is to play another sport...like soccer. Good day, sir."

As a player, you don't come in trying to change the system, you just be the best player you can under the current system's infrastructure. We can't come to God complaining about the spiritual laws that govern this world. They are His laws. We can only play within the parameters given to us. We can't say God isn't real just because death takes our loved ones away. I know it might hurt, but you knew they had to die someday. I used to be fearful of my parents dying, but I had to let them go and give them back to the Father in a spiritual sense. He created them and ultimately they belong to Him. It would be selfish of me to be mad at God when they die. I know they have to leave this earth eventually, so I would rather tell God, "thank you for allowing me time with them while they are here." Because I am conscious of their departure, I try not to waste days with them. We still argue over things, but I try to make amends as soon as I can. Their life is a gift to me, equivalent to a new car or a roof over my head.

I try to stay thankful all around and do right by any gift God gives me. Once you get to a place of thankfulness with God for everything He does, you will receive revelations about the Father and his purpose. For that mother who held her son for only a couple of hours after his birth before he passed away, you were still blessed. I know you might be bitter toward God, but think, some women can't even conceive at all. Even though his life was cut short, you were able to look your son in the eyes and tell him that you love him, and if the Word of God is true, you will see your son again in eternity. That mother who didn't conceive doesn't have a son or daughter to greet them at the gates. Again, you are blessed, my sister.

You might be in a place to where you don't want to hear this, but it's true. As for the reader who might have been the victim of some type of evil, we can't let the enemy put doubt in our brains about our Lord just because sin is present on earth. We were born in a world doomed since the first sin. Going back to the basketball analogy from earlier, God didn't change the rules to the game. The parameters are still in play. Instead, He added a power play to the existing game. Instead of taking away free will, which essentially is the basis for us acting out our sinful thoughts in the natural, or destroying us all together, He sent His son Jesus to die for us and take the hit. Unlike the NBA commissioner, He altered the game because of your letter. He might not have altered it the way YOU wanted Him too, but He is faithful and true nonetheless. He gave us a way to win in the end. He crafted a beautiful ending to the longest movie ever called *Existence*, but we all want to get up and critique the movie before the climax.

This reference point about salvation can be totally separate, yet still connected to our day-to-day struggle. Even if you asked Jesus to be your personal savior, you could still not listen to the voice of the Lord and struggle for the remainder of your life. You would still go to heaven, you just wouldn't have the peace of the Lord and walk in His blessing while on this earth. Ephesians 1:13-14 reads, "In Him you also trusted, after you heard the word of truth, the gospel of your salvation; in whom also, having believed, you were sealed with the Holy Spirit of promise, who is the guarantee of our inheritance until the redemption of the purchased possession, to the praise of His glory." God is so faithful that instead of leaving us to walk blindly through the fog, He left us with a physical guide called the bible, and a spiritual guide called the Holy Spirit. These two helpers are your voices of truth, one in the spiritual and one in the natural realm. They were placed here with specific missions to release the lives of the ones who seek the revelation.

Let's connect the dots by starting at the end and working backward. It will soon make sense. Some Christians say they worship the Lord, but don't ever know when He is speaking to them. Non-believers don't believe in the Lord at all, so they most likely aren't looking for God to speak to them. Well then, how does God reveal to His children that He is a living God? How does He reveal to us that He is with us right now? Matthew 7:7 says, "Ask, and it will be given to you; seek, and you will find; knock, and it will be opened to you." Break it down. Ask, and it will be given to you: He reveals himself to ones that ask Him to do so. He marvels at the request to show you who He is. He loves you. Numerous Christians have testimonies of being atheists, devil worshippers, people in bad situations ranging from abuse to incarceration, etc., and at a given time in their lives, they really asked God to reveal Himself to them. They probably didn't do it in a churchy, holier-than-thou way, but genuinely asked God if He was real, to show up. By them now being Christians, you know He did. He always does!

The second part to the scripture is seek, and you shall find: He reveals Himself to ones that seek Him. When I first became saved, it seemed like God was doing David Blaine magic tricks for me. Literally I would pray something simple like, "God, I'm bored. I wish somebody would pick me up to go somewhere. You know I don't have a car." Before I could get the prayer out my mouth, one of my friends would be at the door. Simple requests I sent up to Him in the privacy of my own prayer were sometimes granted instantly. He made sure I knew He was real and that my prayers were worth His attention. I remember telling my mom about how He was answering me and saying, "If this is what it's like to follow Jesus, I'm never leaving." Over time though, that waiting period between my prayers and His answers lengthened. That love I had for God began to change because I wasn't getting what I wanted when I wanted it. One day as I was complaining to Him about how slow He was moving on my behalf, He spoke to me through the Holy Spirit. He revealed an image of me as a child playing in my backyard. I was running around as if I were playing with someone that wasn't there. Then that person must have left because I remember having a feeling of disorientation. Then I heard a voice call my name and say, "come here." I walked a little toward the edge of the yard, but I stopped. I knew that I wasn't allowed to leave that area when I was playing. The voice said, "you have to come find me." Then the image left and I came back to my present state. Not only did I have that visual, but instantly my spirit became super excited about the Word of God. He had placed a zeal in my spirit to seek Him. I didn't just want to read the bible because someone told me to, but I really wanted to seek out who God, Jesus Christ, and the Holy Spirit were as the Holy Trinity. I wanted to know the truth about life, about death, about the ways of the world and the treasures of eternity. I was seeking the same truths that you are probably seeking right now.

Lastly it says knock, and it will be opened to you. Once you ask God to reveal Himself, He will. Then you become curious to see if the revelation is real, and you begin to search. You start praying more, asking God for signs, reading about Him, asking other believers about Him, etc. Once you come to your own conclusion and see God's glory all around you, knock on the door of your heart and it will be opened to you. That knock is receiving Jesus as your personal savior. His love and His teachings will pierce your heart and change you forever. Your heart will be opened to the truth of our purpose of why we were created by God, and why our adoration toward Him is so important. It will all be revealed to the man or woman who asks, seeks, and knocks.

Now you have accepted Jesus Christ as your lord and personal savior, but don't know where to go from here. Let me pose a hypothetical situation to you. Let's say you didn't have a bible near you. Let's say you will NEVER have a bible around you. What would you do? Is your faith attached to the scriptures, which were given by God, or the voice of God itself? They both intertwine but they are separate. If you are being attacked by the traps of Satan and don't have a scripture to reference, you can ALWAYS talk to God. I'm not talking about the thirty-minute prayers you see in churches nowadays. I talk to God the same way I would talk to you on the street. To be honest, if your friend was trapped under a car, would you stop and pray for an extended period of time or would you just say, "God help me," and begin trying to lift the car? Those three words are more than enough. When your husband is having a midlife crisis and you don't have time to run and find your bible, how can God prove to you in that moment that He is real and ready to help you?

John 14:26 says, "But the Helper, the Holy Spirit, whom the Father will send in My name, he will teach you all things, and bring to your remembrance all things that I said to you." God left us a supernatural spiritual Helper to help you in this physical realm. He knew we would not believe fully unless we had some type of physical assistance. The Holy Spirit has helped me on all types of occasions. I have asked for His help when I lost my keys and needed to find them. I have asked for His help to give me the words to speak when one of my friends was contemplating suicide. When looking for the keys, I heard a voice speak and it told me where to search. Next thing you know, I had my keys. When speaking to my friend, the most beautiful words came out that I didn't even know I could say. That's because they weren't my words, they were His.

Many will say that the bible is the main source that we should focus on in the church community, and I halfway agree. It plays a vital role in our growth as Christians, but knowing God's voice is most important. If you talk to Him and can hear Him when He responds, He can reveal things to you, with or without a bible present. In John 5:37-40, Jesus says, "And the Father Himself, who sent Me, has testified of Me. You have neither heard His voice at any time, nor seen His form. But you do not have His word abiding in you, because whom He sent, Him you do not believe. You search the scriptures, for in them you think you have eternal life; and these are they which testify of Me. But you are not willing to come to Me that you may have life." God can reveal, strengthen, and give you hope through the scriptures; but nothing can replace a true relationship with the Father. When I say true, I mean an intimate, "I talk to you daily" relationship. I'm not talking about the "I go to church for two hours, yell really loud, pray until I get lightheaded, quote 8,000 scriptures, then God and I don't speak until next Sunday" relationship.

I truly believe in the power of the Holy Spirit; it's imperative that you know the voice of the Lord, along with the written doctrine within the bible. The bible serves many purposes. It gives us insight on the beginning of creation. It shows us prophecy that was spoken and written about Jesus before He was born. This proves that God has to be real for someone to be able to speak about His Son's coming existence before He walked the earth. The bible also gives us accounts of Jesus' miracles and teachings to show His love for us. It gives us a roadmap to line our hearts and intentions with the will of God. It also gives us a glimpse into the future prophecy. By showing you the earlier prophecies and how they came to pass, it gives us a foundation of faith to believe in the prophecies spoken that have yet to reveal themselves in our present time. He has given us more than enough of the picture to be satisfied, yet somehow we still aren't. However, if you are one that is satisfied, then bring the point full circle. If you believe in what the bible says, then you have to heed God's warnings about the plans of the devil to harm us. The bible clearly shows us that the battle is in the mind. So to defeat the attacks, you have to guard your mind, which means you have to guard your thoughts. If you have a grip on what you dwell upon, putting each thought up against the Word of God to check its purity, then you will be able to call BS on the devil when he tries to hit you with his words of deception. You will know those can't be your thoughts because you don't believe them to be true.

When you start to feel depressed, you can then combat it with the truth that God is not a God of depression. He has a plan to prosper you. You can call him out and say, "Devil, you are a lie." That's how you combat Satan and regain your freedom from his dominion.

Sometimes you might have a pity party, but try not to stay at the party too long.

If you want to feel an emotion, get mad at Satan and become determined to go through the trial with expectancy. Now I know I make this sound so easy. Believe me, it's not. I can wake up, play some Donnie McClurkin or Andy Mineo, and be in such a good mood. I'm walking around my house singing and rapping praises to God, and it feels like it's just Him and me. I leave the house on cloud nine, feeling higher than a fiend that popped two pills. I'm listening to my spirit, doing whatever God asks of me in that moment: quietly praying for people, speaking blessings into people lives, etc. In my mind I'm thinking, "I don't care what Satan throws at me today. I'm in the zone like Michael Jordan." Not even ten minutes later, the enemy unleashes his attack. I might walk up to a counter in a store to ask a question, and the clerk is extremely rude to me. I'm not just talking a little rude, I mean neck rolling, eye popping, lip smacking, "I hate my life, so you will hate yours too" rude. I feel myself about to turn up, and I catch it. The voice of the Holy Spirit is speaking to me saying, "Calm down and be forgiving, C.J. You don't know what she has been through today, or any day." I agree with God's wisdom and proceed with our conversation, looking past her disrespect. Sadly, it not only continues but gets worse. The next thing I know I'm about to black out on her. I still hear the same voice from the Holy Spirit, but this time I'm focused on my emotions instead. I block Him and go in on the clerk. She hears it from me so strong that I'm breathing hard when I'm done. I yell about that attitude of hers and where she can shove it. After the bombs have been dropped and the hostility subsides, I hear the voice again say, "You know you were wrong for that, C.J. Regardless of how she acts, that's not how I taught you to respond." I'm thinking, "She deserved it though, God. She came at me. I was just in a good mood." Then the Holy Spirit convicts me, and shortly after I'm apologizing to this clerk. See how quickly the attacks from the enemy can change a situation?

So again, we have to always be mindful to not let another person's response to his or her own thoughts affect our thoughts and actions. We have to guard our thoughts before they turn into physical manifestations that might be hurtful. I'm not saying that this change will happen in you overnight. Some people feel you should be perfect. They expect you to let people just walk over you without responding. I'm not one of those people. I love the Lord with all my heart, and He knows that. He has done a great work in me so far, and I'm so excited to see what He continues to do. With that being said, the fact remains that He is still working on me. I came up in the streets. I don't like being disrespected, never have. I came up in an era where respect was something you would live and die for... PERIOD! Now I live for the truth of God's word. That thought-changing process takes time. I can't say that if someone comes at me foul, they won't hear about it from me. I'm real about who I am. I don't walk under a false cloak of righteousness, and if I think you do when I meet you, I'm going to reveal it. I'm never fake with God, nor with His people, and He loves me for that. It makes it easier for me to take His correction when He convicts me for my wrongdoings. I'm free from fake judgment, and daily I work to contest the lies from the enemy.

If you don't take anything else from this book, receive this in the name of Jesus: There is NOTHING that can separate you from the love of Jesus Christ, unless you deny Him yourself. If you accept Jesus as your personal savior, you can talk to Him anytime. Sometimes I'm in the middle of watching porn and I get convicted. While the porn is still playing in front of me, I speak to God. "Lord, I know I shouldn't be watching this, but I'm stuck right now. My heart says don't, but I'm hella horny. Can you please help me? I can't get up." Right then someone will call my phone or the internet will freeze up. A note to be made is that these distractions that occur for me are only for a short time. The computer won't break, the page will just freeze up, but I have to decide to not hit the refresh button; or the phone will ring but I still have to get up and answer it. The Lord provides a way out, but I still have to make a decision and move on it. This window of interruption might seem small in the physical realm, but in hindsight, it's more than enough in the spiritual realm. I just needed a break in thought to regain my focus. That focus can be restored by offering up a prayer of thanksgiving to the Lord for helping you at that moment, getting up and leaving the area where the sin is being committed, or just replacing that action with something else. That's the realness of God.

I can't say it enough. He is SO REAL, and He is SO FAITHFUL! Unlike your friends and family, he won't judge you. The only judgment is at the end. As long as you accept Jesus Christ as your personal savior, you're good. That's what the Word of God says, and that's what I believe. That goes for people who are gay and lesbian, murderers, adulterers, pedophiles, gossipers on Facebook, and the list goes on and on. Romans 10:9 reads, "That if you confess with your mouth the Lord Jesus and believe in your heart that God has raised Him from the dead, you will be saved." It doesn't say add to it something like, "and you can have never raped someone." It also says "believe in your heart." What man or woman do you know that can see your heart? Even a surgeon can't see what God is talking about. God knows your heart's desires. You can't hide your motives from Him. Regardless of what the world sees, He knows who you really are and if you have ill intent for

His word. Some still might disagree with that statement. Their homes don't have mirrors so they can't see themselves.

Sin is sin. No matter if you are a man that's more gay than *Brokeback Mountain*, or a man that has more female sexual partners than Wilt Chamberlain, it's all sin to God. He knew we couldn't be perfect, so He sent Jesus, the perfect lamb, to be sacrificed for us. Every time someone throws your sin in your face, they are really just telling you why Jesus came to die for you. He bore that cross on Calvary for our sins so we don't have to. Before you get all crazy, thinking I'm saying it's cool to sin, I'm not. I'm just saying that God loves each person specifically, and understands exactly where he or she is in his or her life.

Romans 6:15-19 states,

> What then? Shall we sin because we are not under law but under grace? Certainly not! Do you not know that to whom you present yourselves slaves to obey, you are that one's slaves whom you obey, whether of sin leading to death, or of obedience leading to righteousness? But God be thanked that though you were slaves of sin, yet you obeyed from the heart that form of doctrine to which you were delivered. And having been set free from sin, you became slaves of righteousness. I speak in human terms because of the weakness of your flesh. For just as you presented your members as slaves of uncleanness, and of lawlessness leading to more lawlessness, so now present your members as slaves of righteousness for holiness.

That gay minister, who you say on Tuesday is an abomination of God, might be freed from her bondage on

Wednesday and not be gay anymore. Or she might not ever change, and forever battle that demon which tells her the lie that she was created to be gay. Point is, it's not for you and me to pass judgment on anybody, not even on ourselves. We are to let the Holy Spirit correct and guide us.

God will send people that will speak His words to you about certain things going on in your life. Those words won't be of hate and finger pointing; they will be of love because the Father is love. That love might be truthful tough love, because the Word of God cuts deeply to the soul. God also is a God of wrath, but that's HIS wrath. He chooses how to deal with us, so leave it up to Him. He hasn't given any of us the power to do His job. If you are a weed smoker, while you are taking a hit from the blunt, tell God thank you that in due time He will take that away from you. Don't focus on people telling you that YOU have to change. God is the only one that changes us. This same God is the creator of our universe. You think he can't take that away from you in His time? You just trust that God is working on your behalf. You will be cleansed and exalted.

Proverbs 3:5-6 states, "Trust in the Lord with all your heart, and lean not on your own understanding. In all your ways acknowledge Him, and He shall direct your paths." The world might be focused on you smoking weed because they can see it, but God might be healing something totally different in you internally. Dealing with your weed smoking habit might be way down on His priority list. He could be working on your anger, but you're concentrating on trying to stop smoking because another person dogged you about it. Because you are adjusting yourself to the words of man instead of the Word of God, you continue to get frustrated and agitated. This translates to you becoming angrier, which is total opposite of what He's trying to mend in your spirit, and the devil wins. Wake up, people. Two Corinthians 5:7 says, "For we walk by faith, and not by sight." We have to start praying for people instead of running up to them and feeling like we are Super Christians and beating them in the face with the bible. The Holy Spirit will do what He is commissioned to do. He will change you inwardly and it will reflect outwardly.

We have to have faith in this process. We have to have faith that the Holy Spirit is competent and capable. He was given to us by the Father in Jesus' name to help us; we weren't given to the Holy Spirit to help Him. Faith is, and always has been, the cornerstone of our belief. Even for believers who, without a doubt, know they are going to heaven, they still have to have faith on the matter. God didn't send us a physical hand-written invitation that guarantees our salvation. We have to believe what He says is true. Ephesians 2:8 says it perfectly, "For by grace you have been saved through faith, and that not of yourselves; it is the gift of God." That's why He shows Himself to us while on earth so we can have a true belief and expectancy for our new home after we pass away from this world. He blesses us with things like success and family because we are His children, but ultimately salvation for our lives and having an intimate relationship with each and every one of us is His main goal. Just focus on your communication with Christ, and ask God to help you change to be more like Him. Galatians 5:16 speaks, "I say then: Walk in the Spirit, and you shall not fulfill the lust of the flesh." Just trust in the power of the Holy Spirit. The devil is always trying to get our focus away from the truth, even when we are seeking God to know what that truth entails. This is war and He wants to confuse us to where we are fighting one other.

Sometimes even our foundational process for developing a relationship with Christ begins with deception from the enemy.

When you become saved, it's such a pivotal moment in your life. You become Neo from the Matrix, choosing the red or blue pill. God begins to show you the truth about many things going on around you. He'll reveal things within yourself, good and bad, that you didn't even know existed. Then somewhere along your walk, it quits being about the intimacy. You quit reading the bible because it's God's word that brings understanding and revelation into your life. You read it because they say that's what Christians do. You read it because you are ashamed of your lack of knowledge when you are around other "well-versed" Christians. You let fear set in and the next thing you know, you're memorizing 1,000 scriptures so you can have something to quote at the next bible study class. Memorizing scriptures is always a good thing, but what's your motive? Is it so you're able to speak life back to the devil when he surrounds you with thoughts of death? Or is it so that you can get your "Sister Jenkins sure knows her word; she knows everything" praise from your fellow man? There are so many things that we do just because we see other people do them. None of these things were given to you specifically in the Spirit, even if they are spiritual things.

For example, you could be reading your bible and God keeps telling you to read the book of Romans. For two days straight, you have been prompted by the Holy Spirit to read through this particular book, but instead you spend that time memorizing scriptures for your bible study class. You justify it by saying to yourself, "It's all God's word. I will be better equipped to help someone and myself, because I will know these scriptures verbatim." So to you, it's still Godly. Little did you know, the Holy Spirit was prompting you to read this particular piece in the bible for two days because God knew that a co-worker of yours was going to speak to you about Him on the third day.

The co-worker starts off with normal conversation, but soon it switches over to a certain topic. He is on the fence about being a believer, but he doesn't agree with some of the things that go on in church. He tells you that he went one time long ago, and the preacher was putting on a show while his devout followers were all falling on the ground. It disturbed him. He also says that the minister made him feel like if he didn't believe in all of the rituals the church was doing, then to not come back. Now here you are, knowing God gave you a chance to witness. You've been praying all week that God would send you someone that you could minister to. You start quoting all these scriptures that you learned but it seems they aren't having an effect. You are somewhat confused at this moment; therefore, you begin to pray that God helps you tell this man something that can help him. Of course God is faithful, and He gives you a generic word to speak. Your co-worker feels slightly better and tells you thank you for talking. He wasn't completely feeling the answer you gave, but it was enough for him to feel comfortable to come back later if he needed to.

You sit at your desk and cry out to God, "Why did it feel like that didn't go properly? God, it just doesn't feel right in my spirit. I was supposed to speak more to him." You might even start to kind of second guess your relationship with God, thinking He didn't hear you when you asked for His help. Later you go to your bible study class, still thinking about what happened earlier. Afterward, you talk with another church member, explaining what happened with your co-worker. Instead of giving you his personal answer, he grabs your hand and says, "Let's pray about it together." He prays a very short but genuine prayer, asking God to reveal to both you and your co-worker what His will is for this particular situation. Then he tells you to wait and listen for the Holy Spirit to answer you, no matter how long it takes. You get home and finally settle down. Again you get this prompting from the Holy Spirit to read the book of Romans. This time you have nothing to do, so you oblige the request.

Forty-five minutes later you read Romans 4:1-5, "What then shall we say that Abraham our father has found according to the flesh? For if Abraham was justified by works, he has something to boast about, but not before God. For what does the scripture say? Abraham believed God, and it was accounted to him for righteousness. Now to him who works, the wages are not counted as grace but as debt. But to him who does not work but believes on Him who justifies the ungodly, his faith is accounted for righteousness." You instantly light up. You know that the scriptures are saying that Abraham was not justified by the things he did, meaning his works. God made a promise to Abraham, and Abraham trusted Him to fulfill it. Because of Abraham's faith, God credited him with righteousness. He didn't gain this righteousness from God because he obeyed the law, or was performing rituals. He simply believed in God. God gives righteousness to those who believe. The person who doesn't work, who comes to God by faith alone without performing rituals or following "church laws," that person will be counted righteous because of his belief. Now you tell God thank you, ecstatic for tomorrow so that you can share this with your co-worker.

Going back to what was spoken earlier, it's not wrong to do things like memorizing scriptures to become a better Christian. It's needed, actually. When you do these things though, you have to make sure your motives are correct. We all move on our own accord and ignore the voice of the Holy Spirit at times. You were more focused on what you wanted to do, which was memorizing the scriptures for bible study class. You heard and felt God tell you specifically to read Romans at that given time, but you chose the churchy route. You would much rather have been prepared for bible study class, because you knew that people would talk about you if you weren't. Even though what you were doing wasn't a bad thing, God had a specific mission for you to carry out. This "You," individual I'm speaking of, happened to be me.

That's why God kept telling me to make sure I could hear his voice. What if that man died that night, and that was his moment to give his life to Christ? I would have missed the mark because I didn't follow the voice of the Lord. The devil could have possibly claimed another soul because I was too focused on doing my own thing. Not to mention, that "thing" I was doing (memorizing scriptures), was mostly fueled because of my fear to be ridiculed by my peers. That would mean the devil kept me from my moment because of one of his deception war tactics. It was never about the action per se (memorizing the scriptures), but instead it was about Satan blinding me with my own "apple." He hit me with the same strategy that he used on Eve. My apple was fear. I was so focused on not looking bad in front of people. Though God had given me an order, I didn't follow it. Praise God that He revealed it to me again so that I could speak life to my co-worker's situation. So I reiterate to you, and to myself, to just take one step at a time. As long as we continue to progress in our relationship with the Lord, not allowing Satan to make us stop and give up, we will be okay. Keep moving by the Holy Spirit, in step with Jesus.

Put your confidence in Jesus.

What does that really mean to you? The Merriam-Webster dictionary defines "confidence" as:

a) A feeling or belief that one can do something well or succeed at something.
b) A feeling or belief that someone or something is good or has the ability to succeed.
c) A feeling or belief that something will happen or that something is true.

So to say that you are truly putting your confidence in Jesus, you are saying:

a) I put my belief in Jesus (that he can do something well or succeed at something) for me.
b) I put my belief in Jesus (that He is good and/or He has the ability to succeed) for me.
c.) I put my belief in Jesus (that something will happen and/or that it will be true) for me.

Now think back to the latest issue that demanded your attention. When things didn't pan out the way you wanted them to, what did you do? When you didn't get that job you applied for, what was your response? Did you focus on God's promise to you in Jeremiah 29:11? "For I know the thoughts I think toward you, says the Lord, thoughts of peace and not of evil, to give you a future and a hope." Or did you focus on the situation, trying to get a solution by any means necessary? Now before I go on my soapbox about how we should live with confidence in Jesus, I wanted to go another route. Maybe somebody is reading this book thinking they haven't lost confidence in Jesus, when in reality they have, just not fully.

It is true that the bible says in Matthew 17:20 that "if you have faith as a mustard seed, you will surely say to this mountain, 'Move from here to there,' and it will move; and nothing will be impossible for you." God doesn't require enormous amounts of faith from you to do His job. A car doesn't need an abundance of gasoline in it to get it started. It does, however, need more gas for longer trips. In Luke 13:19, Jesus states that the kingdom of God is like "a mustard seed, which a man took and put in his garden; and it grew and became a large tree, and the birds of the air nested in its branches." A tree of the mustard family would grow to about twelve feet in stature. That's a pretty big tree, and to think it started from a seed that's no bigger than a point on the end of a pencil.

God will work with ANY amount of faith you have to offer up to Him. He is also a great and patient teacher, like Mr. Miyagi in *The Karate Kid*. He will groom you with lessons shown by the Holy Spirit so that your faith increases with each revelation and victory. This is how your confidence in Jesus will be built. It will be a tangible thing that you won't be afraid to announce to the world. You won't just say you wholeheartedly believe in Him out of fear of being criticized as the Christian that deep down might not believe. He doesn't want your fake praise. Why would I go out in public and proclaim that Jay-Z saved my house from going into foreclosure if he didn't? Why would I say *That 70s Show* is a great show if I've never seen it before? (Which I have, and it's extremely funny.)

It's one thing to just say, "God is definitely blessing me. I have a job, healthy family, a roof over my head, etc." He understands your thankfulness for Him providing in your life, but think about some of the encounters in the bible that we build our faith upon. Stories like Daniel in the lion's den, David and Goliath, Moses and the Red Sea, they all were supernatural occurrences that seem far-fetched when read. Non-believers and believers alike agree at times that these things seem unrealistic. Do you know that there are miracles of that magnitude still happening? People on this earth are experiencing real life manifestations of God's ultimate power while the rest of us, by our own choice, are still riding with training wheels. If you really look at God in the bible, He always was personal with His people. He always exalted them in front of others. He always did supernatural and unexplainable things. He ALWAYS made sure we, as His creations, knew who He was and what He could do.

So why would you think that what you are reading is so beyond the twenty-first century? Did God start taking smoke breaks? Did He leave work early? The answer is No. We have lost our confidence in what's unnatural. He wants to do things in your life that are so unreal, that you will boldly and proudly tell anyone what just happened. If some random stranger took a bullet for you, how many of us would tell that honorable story? We do it every day when we speak about our men and women who serve in our various branches of the military. We will show pictures of our family to random strangers, drive around the world with a "my child is on the 'A' honor roll" bumper sticker on the back, selfishly brag about ourselves to others, yet when we are able to give a testimony, we get generic. The devil continues to blind us from the truth by masquerading it. He has gotten the world so numb to where we downplay everything. We can't even see the glory in God's magnificent work to be able to tell anyone. How then can we have confidence in our King? God wants to show you today that the devil has been keeping you from your true potential by limiting your faith.

Let me give you two testimonies, one minor and one extreme, that will give you an idea of what God has done in my life to give me confidence in Him. I'll start with the minor one first. So God was working on my selfishness when it comes to money. I grew up with a father that literally worked his way up from ashy to classy. He is one of sixteen siblings (I know right, my grandmother gets my respect for all those childbearing years). He mostly had hand-me-downs growing up. So when he was able to provide for his family, he was always tight with money. You would have to kill him before he would loosen that grip on his income. That same tightness trickled down to me.

During my six years in the military, I started a multimedia company called Lucid Bleu Entertainment. At the early stages of building the company, I used to get so mad at God because I felt He wasn't blessing my work fast enough. I just kept praying, "Give Me, Give Me, Give Me." Finally God spoke to me saying, "If you want Me to bless it, YOU need to give more." Initially I was upset because that wasn't the response I wanted to hear. As I started to think, though, I realized He was right. When was the last time I "really" helped somebody else instead of always praying for myself?

So God helped me get with a volunteer group called Happy Helpers for the Homeless. I had a blast working with these volunteers. My heart always goes out to people living in those types of conditions. My service there was ongoing, and I was truly blessed in my spirit by helping.

One day while at work for the Army, I asked my fellow co-workers if they could donate clothes to the homeless organization. The turnout was amazing. They really came through and blessed those in need. As I was alone in the office packing up the clothes, I prayed to God, telling Him thank you for this entire adventure He took me on. I told Him that I would have never known how great it would feel to do something of this nature. Before, I was too selfish to really enjoy it.

I then told God that I wanted to do something nice for my co-workers. I knew everybody there wasn't a Christian, yet they still did a Godly act. I wanted them to know that I loved them, and was very appreciative of their help. I was about to make my own decision on what to do; then instead, I asked God. I heard a voice say the number "200" followed by the word "food." I remember looking up and repeating the word "food" with the ugly face. That was the last thing I would have thought to get them. Then He brought back to my memory that my co-workers had skipped lunch because of training we had done earlier. Praise God that He's smarter than me. I had totally forgot. I didn't know what the "200" meant at the time. I worked with about fifty to seventy-five people in my building, so I thought it had something to do with that number. I finished packing the clothes and I decided that I would pick up the food from McDonald's.

As I'm walking toward my car, I hear the Holy Spirit speak again. Not only does He tell me to go to Chick-Fil-A, but a specific location. The one He chose was like ten minutes away. Me being lazy, I start complaining and questioning if I really heard anything. I thought maybe I was just thinking aloud. I stopped in the middle of the parking lot and verbally asked God did I hear the command right. Instantly, my spirit felt warm and the inside of my body lit up. That's the best way I can describe what I felt. So I followed His words and drove past several other restaurants on my way to Chick-Fil-A.

When I walked inside, it was packed. I saw a young guy with a tag that said assistant manager, working one of the registers. I was about to walk up and talk to him, but the Holy Spirit said "No, not him." So I spoke to the young guy and asked him for the manager. He asked if he could help me. I politely said no, and insisted on speaking to his boss. He went to the back and came out with an older lady. I explained how my co-workers were so generous in their giving, and that I wanted to bless them back. She asked me what I wanted to purchase, and I responded "I don't know." She looked at me puzzled. Right then, the Holy Spirit spoke again telling me to spend $200. It made sense now.

Spending $200 was big for me because of how I said earlier that I was tight with money. This was my test to see how I would respond. He brought my entire situation full circle. This time around, I was thankful that the Lord allowed me to be a blessing with the finances He gave me. I looked back at the lady and said "I have $200 to spend on food. Just give me anything." She asked me to repeat the reason I was buying the food, and then told me to hold on. By now, I was still confused about why God told me to come to this particular restaurant. As I sat there waiting for the lady to come back, I became thirsty. I was going to get in line, but it was out the door. I knew by the time I got up, the woman would be back. I started to pout and I spoke to God very sarcastically, "God, it would really be nice to get something to drink right now. That lemonade looks so good. You know I'm trying to do something nice for my people." Right then the lady came back to the front. I got up from my chair and approached her and she told me that the regional manager wanted to speak to me. I looked at her, confused, and asked her, "why?" She said that situations like these are usually handled on the corporate level, but that I had incredible timing. Then she asked, "Do you want something to drink, maybe a lemonade?" My jaw dropped. I knew God was laughing at me.

I still didn't understand what "situation" the lady was referring to, but before I could get clarification, the regional manager came out. He kept asking me which non-profit company I represented. I told him several times that I wasn't affiliated with any non-profit company. I just wanted to spend $200 on food. He finally understood what I was doing and a big smile fell upon his face. He asked how many people I was feeding. I said roughly between fifty and seventy-five people. He rang me up for a large nugget tray, fifty Chick-Fil-A sandwiches, and fifty cookies. The total was over $200. I was going to question him about the amount, but I changed my mind. I knew the man had heard me correctly because I said $200 like fifty times during the conversation. So I just took it as another test from God and let my hands free from the money. When I went to pay, the regional manager said that it was on him. I was blown back. He said the reason he kept asking me which non-profit I was affiliated with was because Chick-Fil-A normally writes off donations during tax time. He said since I was doing a good deed, He wanted to bless me. How BIG is God! Not only that, come to find out, that particular regional manager was prior military. We shook hands and he disappeared in the back of the restaurant.

Now this was the icing on the cake. The lady approached me and said, "I'll say again, you have incredible timing. The regional manager only comes to our store twice a month for a couple of hours. You were RIGHT ON TIME." That's why God wanted me to go to this particular store. Look at the window of time. If I had questioned God's voice any longer, I might have missed my blessing. The Lord saw my heart and gave the blessing back to me at no cost. Hallelujah. That's

God being God. I can tell that story a million times over because I know God arranged that entire series of events.

Another example happened when I was incarcerated. I was placed in one of the worst jails in America, located in the heart of Baltimore. If you want to know how crazy it is, just Google "Baltimore Correctional Detention Center." I was convicted and sentenced to two years in prison, but they suspended a year and nine months on my sentence. I had to serve a mandatory three months in that place. Even with that, I praise God that He kept me from doing the entire two years. I won't go into the situation surrounding why I was locked up, but if you ever meet me, just ask and I will indulge your curiosity.

While I was doing my time, I had to adapt to the rules within. I have always been in the streets. I will not say that I haven't done things that were deserving of jail time, but I had never been arrested up until this point. I was still in the army during this time; therefore, I was trying to keep a low profile. I didn't want to get into a situation and catch another charge. When you're locked up, the best time of the day is when you get to use the phones. The phones are for everyone's use. The thing is though, some of the phones are claimed by the various groups within the jail. These groups only let you use their particular phone if you are affiliated with that group, or get the nod from someone in that group. There was a Muslim phone (only Muslims), a Crypt (gang) phone, a Blood (gang) phone, a Black Guerrilla Family "BGF" (gang) phone, a Spanish Connection (only Spanish gangs) phone, a White Supremacy (KKK-type gang) phone, and two remaining phones for the rest of the population.

When they would let us out of our cells, everybody would rush to the phones. You only get fifteen minute calls, but people would abuse their privilege. They would get their fifteen minute call, then use another fifteen minutes to call someone else. There were fights all the time over the phones. Now when I first went in, I was oblivious to these rules regarding the phones. Some days the lines were too long so I couldn't get a phone call at all. One day they switched me to another cell that was next to a set of phones. So when they let us out later that day, I jetted to the nearest phone to call my wife.

As the phone was ringing, this Haitian-looking guy walked up to me. He said, "This is my phone." At first, because of his accent, I couldn't understand him. I said, "What did you say, big homie?" He repeated himself. While he was talking, my wife picked up the phone. She was so excited to accept the call, that she just started talking as soon as it connected. Between her voice and the guy talking, I still couldn't understand him. He then said "This is Black Guerilla Mafia's phone." Now I got it. I told wifey to hold on and I addressed the guy. I said, "Yo, I'm just calling my wife. I didn't mean any disrespect. I'll make the call short and give you back the phone in a few minutes." Now I know most people would have just hung up the phone—not me. I get in trouble sometimes because I tend to walk in a "no fear" zone. I should have just gotten off of the phone. I let my pride, to a certain degree, kick in.

The guy walked away and I started telling my wife what just happened. As we were speaking, I see that same guy go over to a group of people. He starts to point back at me, and next thing I know, they are all walking swiftly toward me. I told wifey what was happening, and I started to panic a little. I'm a fighter, but the odds were against me. Firstly, there was only one CO (correctional officer) on duty and she was nowhere to be found. Secondly, it was like eight of them and only one of me. Lastly, THIS IS JAIL! People rather shank you, going for the kill, instead of fist fighting. All I could do is pray.

At that very moment I sent up a quick, yet SERIOUS prayer. I said, "God, I need your help." I watched as they got closer. They were anxious for action. Right before they got across the room, God answered my prayer. Normal protocol for an inmate when a CO or a supervisor enters the room is to make a bird call. That gives the other inmates a heads-up to hide their drugs, weapons, or anything of importance. Well, this short, older supervisor had crept in unnoticed. As the guys were approaching me, she was doing random cell checks. Right before they reached me, she had called in that she found a sack of weed in one of the cells. Guess who's cell it was in? Exactly, the guy who initially checked me at the phone. They put us all on the ground, and eventually locked us back down. That guy caught another charge, and they removed him from our area. All his followers were so distraught about what just happened, they left me alone. Again, HOW BIG IS GOD! You can't tell me that was just luck, or a coincidence.

Romans 8:28 reads, "And we know that all things work together for good to those who love God, to those who are called according to His purpose." If you can't see that only God worked that out for me, then I really feel bad for you. He has been so faithful to me in real experiences. I wouldn't call on the name of Jesus, or any other name for that matter, if I didn't believe that it would work. Situations like these are what my confidence in Jesus is built upon. He has shown Himself to me, time and time again.

You have to know fear and doubt will come.

We must stand up and declare, "I won't give up! God knows what I am going through. He loves me, and He is walking through it with me." Trust me, I understand how scary it is at times to truly trust God. I'm telling you, His power is real. Think about if you were starting a company. It's hard growing from the ground up. To make your company successful, you would need loyal people. Like Facebook, you decide to pay your initial employees with stock options. You don't have extra capital to pay them monetary checks at the moment. You need that money to move the company forward. You tell your employees that if they weather the storm with you, at the end they should all be wealthy. They can cash in their stock options at any time, but it would benefit them more to focus on making the company successful. That way they get a higher return on their investment.

Now of course your employees are going to start off super excited. The possibility of being a millionaire clouds their brains. They hit the pavement hard, working around the clock. Then all of a sudden the company's profits start to head toward the red. Your employees begin to panic, thinking all their hard work was for nothing. They are about to lose it all. At this very moment, as the owner, what do you need? Do you need money? Not necessarily. Do you need business advice? Again, not necessarily. What you do need, without a doubt, is loyalty and trust. You knew it was going to be a bumpy road when you decided to start the business. You also knew if everyone made it through the storm, there would be a pot of gold waiting on the other side. As an owner, you know that to be successful, your employees have to trust you through the good and bad times. They have to possess faith that you will bring the ship through the tumultuous waters.

God is the owner of the company called "The Kingdom." God wants you to trust Him through the good and bad times, but especially when it gets bad. It's easy to tell God you trust Him when your job is paying you over $100,000 a year. What about when you only have twenty dollars left to your name, and you owe a hundred and twenty dollars on your light bill? Can you really sit still and trust that God will make a way? Even if your breakthrough doesn't come until the hour before the bill is due? The enemy wants you to say "no." Satan wants you to start making your own decisions without waiting on God. He knows how weak we are without the help of God. He'll pump your head up with all kinds of nonsense, letting you feel like you are in control. We have to be more like Christ and take a stand during the trial or temptation. I really mean it when I say "we." I need help more than most. Even as I write, the Holy Spirit is convicting me of times I didn't trust the words of my Father in heaven. The enemy is always waiting for a crack in your armor so he can attack you. Also, we have to acknowledge that we are not always led into temptation by the devil. It will definitely be the enemy that tempts you, but God can allow that to happen to show you your heart at that very moment. Hate them or love them, trials build up your faith.

Remember in Matthew 4:1-11, when Jesus was led by the Spirit into the wilderness to be tempted by the devil? After fasting for forty days and forty nights, Jesus was starving. The enemy came to Him and said, "If You are the Son of God, command these stones to become bread." Jesus hit him with a scripture, saying "It is written, Man shall not live by bread alone, but by every word that proceeds from the mouth of God." There was nothing morally wrong with turning stones to bread. Satan was tempting Jesus to do a miracle outside of the will of God. Jesus knew that bread alone does not sustain life, but that ultimately God is the one who sustains us. Right there he showed us that it's our responsibility to trust God and remain in His will, regardless how enticing the temptation.

Next, the devil took Jesus into the holy city, set Him on the pinnacle of the temple, and said to Him, "If You are the Son of God, throw yourself down." Then Satan hit Jesus with a scripture, telling Him, "For it is written, He shall give His angels charge over you. In their hands they shall bear you up, lest you dash your foot against a stone." Again Jesus replied with a scripture, saying, "It is written again, You shall not tempt the Lord your God." Satan was quoting to Jesus the protective promise of Psalms 91:11. He purposely omitted a part of the scripture. It should read, "For He shall give His angels charge over you, *TO KEEP YOU IN ALL YOUR WAYS*. In their hands they shall bear you up, lest you dash your foot against a stone." The devil tempted Jesus to gain public attention through spectacle rather than through His righteous life and message. Then, Satan so deviously left out the truth-revealing part of the scripture he spoke.

How often are we tempted in the same manner today? How many times do you hear a voice tell you to go tell someone what the bible says about their wrongdoing, as if you are the bible police? For every scripture you quote that speaks death against sinners, I can find ten that speak grace and forgiveness to the one willing to receive it. It's crazy how the enemy can even use God's precious words to separate the same people that were given the Word to help them. Something to think about.

Lastly, the devil took Jesus up on an exceedingly high mountain and showed Him all the kingdoms of the world and their glory. He told Jesus, "All these things I will give You if You fall down and worship me." That was the straw that broke the camel's back. Jesus told the enemy, "Away with you Satan! For it is written, 'You shall worship the Lord your God, and Him only you shall serve.'" Then the devil left, and angels came and ministered to Jesus. Here are some key points to take from this. Jesus and the devil debated through their words, but the war was for Jesus' actions. Like we agreed earlier, the battle is in the mind.

For example, you and your wife have an argument. While you're full of anger, the enemy comes to you and tells you to find another wife. Instead of stopping the thought right then, you actually contemplate it. Now that he has your attention, he speaks to you, "Just leave and go kick it. She doesn't care about you, so go find someone else that will. I know you're tired of her sex anyway. This is your time to go out and get someone new. You deserve it. F--K her!" Deep down you know these words aren't from the Holy Spirit. You know this isn't what God wants you to do, but you feel the marriage is unsalvageable. Next thing you know, you're listening to

Jay-Z's "On To The Next One," feeling pumped up as you go out for a night of what we call "leave it in the streets." You have sex with a chick that night, but get a phone call the next morning. It's your wife. She really wants to work it out. You don't believe it will get better this time, but you go home and try anyway. Lord behold, God helps you two have a breakthrough. Not only are you not frustrated anymore, but you're actually beginning to be happy about being married. Just when everything you have been praying for in your marriage is starting to be answered, you get contacted by the female you slept with that night. She's pregnant.

Now look back at that entire situation. When you were initially upset with your wife, you left. You didn't just leave the house, you mentally left the relationship. Your anger made you feel in need, the same way Jesus probably felt He needed food when the devil came to Him. Unlike Jesus, you made your own decision instead of inquiring of God's wise council. You could have said to yourself, "I know she is a handful, but I did say for better or for worse. I made a vow before God, so let me try to work it out." If you feel that is too cliché and not realistic, then at least admit that deep down, all men know not to go around women when they are mad at their lady. You could have gone somewhere else instead. The devil never forced Jesus to do anything, but instead, he cowardly played the background while forcefully suggesting that Jesus commit the sins against God. Satan didn't make you go out, actively seeking a woman to be with that night. He just spoke into your Spirit because you received his words to be reality. They were only words; your actions made them reality. Every sin that was committed, was committed by you. You can cry out to God explaining why you did it, but ultimately it was done by you.

Lastly, Jesus rebuked Satan, and he left. Then God sent angels to minister to Jesus. Just like Him, we too have the power to make the devil flee. That's the purpose of this book.

God just wants me to equip people with the proper technique to fight the temptations of the world. That way there will be no excuses. All Jesus did was BOLDLY speak the Word of God back to the devil while He was in a vulnerable state.

When the devil attacks, sometimes you don't feel like fighting back. You are in a bad place and just want to accept his words of condemnation. Don't do it. We have to fight to the end. We mean so much to the Father, and He has done plenty for you and I. Why would you not fight for the truth? I would rather die believing the truth in the promises of the Lord, then to live in the misery of condemnation from the lies spoken by the enemy. That's real talk. You know that old adage, "If you don't stand for something, you'll fall for anything."

Also, the devil approached Jesus when He was down. You know how you feel when you haven't eaten anything for several hours. Just think about how Jesus felt, refraining from eating for over a month. Satan always comes to you at your low points in life. He'll come during the highs too, but be assured that he will definitely come during the rough times. When Satan spoke, Jesus used God's words against the devil's temptation. He couldn't have stood on His belief in the words of God unless He truly believed them to be true. We can't withstand the attacks from the enemy unless you know what you know to be true. Satan is extremely cunning. He used God's word to try and manipulate Jesus. Again, you have to admit that's mind-blowing. It's one thing to just speak negative things to a person, but it's crazy to think that Satan will go as far as using God's righteous word to do his evil bidding.

So let me reiterate the point I wrote just a few lines up. For all you Christians reading this book that use certain parts of the bible to condemn your fellow men and women for the decisions they are making on this earth, really make sure that the Holy Spirit led you to speak to them at that given time. That's why it is imperative that we know the voice of the Lord. We have to strive to be led by the Holy Spirit at all times. Again,

I'm not saying you will make this journey in one day, but this will help you know which direction to walk, and also what you are walking toward. I'm telling you, this is an ongoing war. You need to get your mind right, and do it right now. Lose the bitter taste of religion and come drink from Jesus' everlasting waters. Don't be so focused on God's people, and all their religious rules that they enforce, that you miss the fact that Jesus died for all those things. Accept Jesus, if you truly believe in Him, and let God deal with the rest.

I do want you to live a life pleasing to God, but most importantly, I want you to be saved. There is a prostitute reading this that is feeling extremely unworthy of God's grace because several Christians have told you that you are a disgrace. Sweetheart, accept Jesus into your life. He loves you more than all the Christians in the world put together. We can never love you the way He does. People are worried about what you do as a profession, but God isn't. Jesus kicked it with prostitutes. If you are curious about how it went down, go find a bible and read Luke 7:36-50. It will change your life. I love you, my sister. Be blessed. The Holy Spirit told me to write that for you, so there is a reason in God's purpose. You never know, that next John you service may take your life. I'm praying for your safety in the name of Jesus. God is able. We should give God the glory for our freedom of thinking.

Remember strange storms always precede great miracles.

God is teaching all of us at the same time. Sometimes you gotta wait on your prayer being answered because He is working on someone else's heart. Think about a porn star, for example. When God looks at her, He sees His daughter. He sees the unfinished answer to one of His son's prayers. There is a man right now that is lonely. He has been controlling his sexual urges, but He doesn't know how long he can hold on. He yearns for companionship and prays daily for God to bring him his future wife. That great woman he is asking God to bring him is that porn star. We, the people, see her actions and feel some type of way. To some women, she might be disgusting. They turn their nose up at her speaking as they walk by, "She's the type of woman that gives us REAL WOMEN a bad name." The only time these same women show some type of emotion, other than distaste, is if they find out the porn star's "story of tragedy." If she was raped at age eight, or thrown out into the streets at thirteen, then a flood of great sympathy washes over the ones who judge her.

But what if none of those things happened? What if she was just a very curious and sexual person that took her passions way too far? Without a traumatic event attached, do we just write her off as damaged goods? Think about how many people speak negatively into her life without a care. Every time words of the enemy are spoken at her through people, she has to choose to denounce or accept them. She might not even be a follower of Christ, and if that is true, what promises will she hold onto before she self-destructs? Now, I know many of you reading said in your brain, "I know she's not a follower of Christ. If she was, she wouldn't be a porn star." If you did think that, just tell God sorry for your judgment. If you say, "No, I'm right," then let me let you in on a little dialogue I had with Christ about this topic of "righteousness;" then I'll finish my point about the porn star.

I asked God was He sure I was the one He wanted to write this book? I told him that I didn't want to speak about Him and then do something in the media limelight that would reflect poorly back to my Savior. I love God with all my heart, but that same heart lusts, curses, rejects, quits, etc. My actions don't always match my values, but my values match the Word of God. I told Him, "I don't think I'm ready to represent you because I don't think nor act like other Christians." As I waited for Him to answer, He spoke to me in the Spirit saying, "C.J., tell me what level of 'religious living' constitutes that you're ready?" He said, "How clean does a person have to be before they can talk about the love of Jesus Christ?" He said, "I didn't die for you to have to still get right. I died so you could seek me at any given moment, and I'll be there." Then He hit me hard saying, "When was this 'Christian life' ever about you, C.J.?" I just put my head down. He said, "You are a light, but I am the source. I am your Father. Kids can't chastise kids. And if ANYBODY says something about my child, I will come see them."

So going back to the porn star, all these things she endures creates a storm in her life. Every time she goes to work to have sex, she feels conflicted. She knows that she loves the sex, maybe even the craziness of how they do it, but deep down she feels that she should be giving herself to someone she loves. She is seeking, as the bible would say, but we only see what she has found. We don't know what she prays about, we just feel "If she were a Christian, she would stop." And Lord forbid, this same porn star actually comes to church. Most members would gossip throughout the entire service about her, not even listening to God's word. Then afterward, they would probably try to baptize her in heavy-duty holy water while speaking in tongues for like eight hours. LOL.....They would want to get the demon out of her like it's *The Blair Witch Project*.

What part of any of this is direction from the Holy Spirit? How do we know that God doesn't have a miracle around the corner for this porn star? We don't. Just as easily as God accepted the criminal on the cross, He can accept her. He didn't even question the criminal's past. He knew his heart. The gift of having a heart to please a man sexually, which God gave the porn star, the devil tried to make perverse. But what if she finally found her mate and they got married? What if her husband never judged her line of work because He saw God in the gift He gave him? He can see God's fruits in her, like how loving and unselfish she is, or how she cares about people, even when those same people talk down to her. She tells him that she has always been curious about Christ, but most people shy away from her like she has cancer because of her career choice. He never responds with "what the bible says," but instead just speaks about how good God is for sending His son Jesus to die for us. Next thing you know, she gets saved. Now not only do we have a new member in the body of Christ, you have one that knows the porn business very well. God can soon send her back into that battlefield because she knows the terrain. There are many in that same arena that are seeking, they just haven't told anybody.

That sin you beat yourself up over may be the same sin that you can help someone else be released from. So think about this great transformation that took place in the porn star's life. In the end, most Christians would say, "Praise God for He is worthy. He changed my sister in Christ for the better, and for that I say thank you Jesus…" So go back to the beginning when you didn't know how the story would play out. Would you have been one of the people that walked by and judged her, or would you have extended a helping hand to just love her? What would Jesus have done in that situation? So if you were one of the ones who made that judgment statement earlier, I pray that you can hopefully now see the difference. Anytime we seek to know the truth, it tends to get dirty. Some of the men and women reading this are great spouses only because they almost destroyed the lives of their previous mates. They learned from their mistakes and now they appreciate the gift that God has given them. Now think about if the Holy Spirit prompted you, and you were able to share that testimony with someone God sent you. It would cause you to be vulnerable and show that you're not perfect, but that realness would negate the falseness of the devil and his lies. Every day we have to move past what is normal, routine.

We have to look for the supernatural.

We can't even start this process until we acknowledge how NATURAL we are. Too many of us walk around like we don't need Jesus. Where's the passion? Look at a third world country where the citizens really need food. Those individuals will go to great lengths to get that food. It's necessary for survival. They aren't ashamed, even when sometimes, as Americans, we feel they should be. They do things that we tell ourselves, "I would NEVER do that." How many of you would eat out of a trash can or food that has been on the ground for days? The reader might think, "That would never happen to us, so what's your point?" The point is their desire to find their source of life in the natural, should be surpassed by our passion to seek our source of life in the spiritual.

In Mark 8:22, a blind man was brought to Jesus to be healed. They begged Jesus to touch him. He took the blind man and led him out of the town. Jesus spit on the man's eyes and placed His hands on him. He asked him if he saw anything. The man looked up and said, "I see men like trees walking." Then Jesus put His hands on his eyes again and made him look up. The man was restored and saw everything clearly. So let's place this event in the proper perspective. This man was blind for God knows how long. Think about how badly he wanted to see. He went through life hearing people describe things they were seeing, yet he couldn't visualize them. He could have been mad at God, or just given up all hope, accepting his situation. We don't even know if he truly believed that Jesus could heal him. Nonetheless, he went to go see the master. When the people begged Jesus to heal the man, Jesus took him away outside the town. If put in that same situation, most of us would have been complaining already. With our feeling of entitlement, I could see us saying, "You're Jesus. You can heal people without even touching them. Why do I have to walk somewhere with You?" "Plus you know I can't see anything.

Where are you taking me?" Then Jesus spits on the guy's eyes. How disrespectful is that? Or how faithful is that? By this time, we would be going crazy. We would be cursing and irrationally swinging our fists in the air, because we still can't see. Think about how much this guy wanted to be healed. He took another man's spit to the face, believing in His power instead of focusing on the actions that manifested His power. Then when Jesus asked him the first time if He saw anything, his vision was halfway clear. We would've given up by now, storming off calling Jesus a fake, and a few other choice words. That gentleman stayed through the process to see it through. Some say the guy's lack of faith initially hindered the process. We really don't know the reason Jesus did it twice. To be honest, it doesn't matter why. The fact is the blind man let God do a supernatural healing to his natural body. That man had every reason to doubt that an hour from when he would meet Jesus, he would be able to see EVERYTHING. The devil makes us quit to soon before the supernatural miracle occurs. He sometimes makes us quit during the miracle.

Take Peter, for example. In Matthew 14:22-33, the disciples where settled in a boat located in the middle of the sea. During the night, Jesus came to them by walking on top of the sea waters. When the disciples saw Jesus from afar, they didn't know it was Him. They became fearful. Jesus spoke to them, telling them to be of good cheer, for it was Him. Peter responded, "Lord, if it is You, command me to come to You on the water." Peter didn't just take it upon himself to get out the boat and start walking on the water. He told Jesus to command him to come. This shows Peter acknowledging his natural state so that he could have a supernatural encounter with Jesus in the spiritual realm. Jesus just replied, "Come." There wasn't an hour long prayer session between these two, Jesus just said one command and it was done. Keep that in mind next time you pray.

So Peter got out of the boat and began to successfully walk on the water. Then the winds became boisterous and he became afraid. He started to sink. Immediately, he cried out to the Lord for help. Jesus stretched out His hand and said, "O you of little faith, why did you doubt?" Jesus didn't lose His power; Peter lost His focus. He took his faith off of the power of Jesus and focused on the storm around Him. We have to always remain focused on Jesus, no matter our current situation. Then when he began to sink, he called on the name of Jesus for help. He could have been prideful and tried to swim back to the boat through the rough tide. Instead, he acknowledged his natural need for Jesus' help, and got just that.

Let's go over to Moses now. When Moses was in the mountains, hiding from the wrath of Pharaoh, the Angel of the Lord appeared to him. He said he saw the oppression of His people in Egypt, and had come to deliver them from the Egyptians. God could have just destroyed the Egyptian people with His own might, but instead He said He would send Moses to bring His people out of Egypt. Moses kept it real. He replied to God, "Who am I that I should go to Pharaoh, and that I should bring the children of Israel out of Egypt?" It would seem that Moses was speaking on his abilities from a lack of faith standpoint. To some degree, that is correct. For him to focus on his own abilities as the "entire key" to his success, he was wrong. Yet, within that same statement, he was right. He was also stating that he was just a "natural man." He didn't have an army, superpowers, or anything of the sort to complete the task at hand. He was dead on with his assessment. God replied, "I will certainly be with you. And this shall be a sign to you that I have sent you: When you have brought the people out of Egypt, you shall serve God on this mountain." God greeted Moses' incapacity with His ability. He never asks you to do anything that you're not capable of doing. The key is, everything He asks of you, He expects to walk with you as you complete it.

God never told Moses, "I'm God, this is your mission, figure that out." He said He would be with him. If you notice, He didn't give Moses any insight on what would happen. He just told him that, as a sign, WHEN you bring the people out of Egypt, you shall serve me on this mountain. God never said the things Moses would endure would be easy, but he told him the end result. He gave Moses the entire revelation of the mission with one word: "when."

Too many times we believe in God's word enough to encourage others, but don't believe His promises apply to us.

Even though Moses was adopted by Egyptian royalty, he was still a Hebrew. As an adult, he was emotionally attached to his own people, and noticed they were being mistreated by his adopted people. Moses saw an Egyptian beating a slave, so he killed him for harming his people. God didn't give Moses the right to kill that man, and we know that. If so, he wouldn't have fled Egypt out of fear. God's direction is true, and His words aren't accompanied by fear. Yet, Moses believed in the laws of God written on his heart to where he knew it wasn't right for those people to be mistreated. So keep that in mind. He was charged in his Spirit to stand up for God's people.

Now later when God met him on the mountain and told Moses to go bring His people out of Egypt, he should have been excited. That same passion for justice was now blessed by God with a specific mission attached to it. He now had a proper way, God's way, to save his people. Instead of receiving this instruction with great joy, Moses felt he wasn't capable of doing the job. He had a heart for God's people, to the point of putting himself in jeopardy for their sake, but he couldn't receive God's plan for his own life. How many times have we spoken a God-given word to people close to us, yet we can't believe God's promises in our own lives? God doesn't lie. He can't lie.

Many of you reading this book have been praying for years about a specific breakthrough. Because you have not seen it manifest itself, you have lost your faith. You might say out of your mouth that you believe, but your fruits say otherwise. Some of you have been praying for a financial gain. The Holy Spirit has prompted you numerous times to start a project. That project could be writing a book, starting a company, helping a specific person, reading your bible more, etc. You tell yourself that you aren't able, but God says, "Child, what can you not do if I am with you? What is there that I, God Almighty, cannot do?" You still believe that God can bless you, but instead of receiving your assignment that will bring deliverance, you rather keep an Egypt mindset. Do you know that the enemy is laughing at you right now? Satan is like, "They're easy targets. I don't even have to physically do anything to deter them. I just speak a few words and they give up. I can't believe God thinks they are His soldiers, His chosen people. My team is winning over here."

Because Satan has our focus off of the war, we feel that there is no need to fight. We feel that when we pray, God should just give us what we ask for right then. Honestly though, what good parent would give his children a gift without making sure it will benefit instead of harm them? Though we are God's children, we often don't believe in a season of preparation for the good gifts of the Lord. Compare your present season of preparation with King David's for a second and see if there are any similarities. God sends His servant Samuel to Jesse the Bethlehemite to bring forth a king. Out of all his sons that "physically looked" more capable to do the job, God chose David to be king based on his heart. In 1 Samuel 16:7, God tells Samuel about David's brother Eliab: "Do not look at his appearance or at his physical stature, because I have refused him. For the Lord does not see as man sees, for man looks at the outward appearance, but the Lord looks at the heart." Praise God for that, my brothers and sisters. Even when we make judgments about what we see in ourselves, or others speak on how they view us, God doesn't see us in that same light. He sees our hearts. So the next time you feel that someone overlooked you for a job, relationship, etc., just know that God's not an idiot. He doesn't make mistakes, and in due time He will exalt you, not man.

One Samuel 16:10-11 reads, "Thus Jesse made seven of his sons pass before Samuel. And Samuel said to Jesse, 'The Lord has not chosen these.' And Samuel said to Jesse, 'Are all the young men here?' Then he said, 'There remains yet the youngest, and there he is, keeping the sheep.'" David's own father had forgotten about him, but God did not. Jesse paraded all his other sons in front of Samuel, not even thinking to call David so that he could get in line. How many of you have seen your co-workers get promoted before you, even though you knew you should have been in the pickings? David, from afar, probably watched all of this happen. How do you think he felt, not knowing what was going on? I'm sure they were loud from excitement. These people weren't rich. If someone came to my father's house and said, "Excuse me Mr. Reed, I just wanted to tell you that God has made your son the next King of England," he would be doing back flips.

People may be passing you right now, but God will never forsake us. Even before David's family knew that God would choose a king from them, He was already grooming David. While the other sons were trying to figure who was next to inherit the kingdom, David was doing kingdom work. He was keeping the sheep. The fact that David was tending the sheep at this particular moment has natural and spiritual significance. In the natural realm, God was already teaching David principles needed to be a king. The number one rule of any person in a leadership position is to take care of and protect the people you lead. There's no leaders without followers.

In 1 Samuel 17:33-36, David was preparing to fight the giant Goliath. King Saul said to David, "You are not able to go against this Philistine to fight with him; for you are a youth, and he a man of war from his youth." David replied, "Your servant used to keep his father's sheep, and when a lion or a bear came and took a lamb out of the flock, I went out after it and struck it, and delivered the lamb from its mouth; and when it arose against me, I caught it by its beard and struck and killed it." David then went on to say, "Your servant has killed both lion and bear, and this uncircumcised Philistine will be like one of them, seeing he has defied the armies of the living God."

On the natural level, David was prepared to fight. God had already prepared him by being with David as he killed the lions and bears that tried to attack his flock. God also prepared David's heart for protecting his people when he would become king. David cared for his animals, constantly putting his life on the line to save theirs. This was a time of preparation for him. It was like practice before the big game. Standing up to Goliath was the moment that only God could have set up. David was confident in his own abilities because He was confident in God's ability to be with him. He still believed the covenant promises from God to be true, regardless of who was his adversary. His actions showed his faith, to the point of possible death coming from the Philistine. David was committed to God, win or lose.

Of course we know that David goes on to defeat Goliath, and later becomes King of Judah, then King of Israel. We can read David's story in its entirety to see where God took him, but think about how he felt going through. He probably couldn't understand why his brothers got to go fight, and he had to stay back and tend the sheep. Even after Samuel ordained him to be the new king, David went right back to herding the sheep. Talk about a quick demotion in responsibilities. See, that's only because we see with our natural eyes. God had David right where he needed to be, so that he could learn. God built a foundation, along with an intimate relationship with David, during that time in his life. That was the only way David was successful when it got tough. He knew, because of what he had gone through already, that he could believe God's promises at ANY time to be true. He had to be prepared for his belief. But it was his belief in God's promise that put him in the proper places to receive His blessing. We can't minister to others unless we hear and believe God's word ourselves. We have the same covenant with God as David.

We must think and speak in agreement with God, and believe it will be.

If you don't mind, I would like to go back to the subject of preparation and how we get our blessings. If you read Genesis 4:17-19, God gives Adam his penalty for eating the forbidden fruit in the garden. He says, "Cursed is the ground for your sake; In toil you shall eat of it all the days of your life. Both thorns and thistles it shall bring forth for you, and you shall eat the herb of the field. In the sweat of your face you shall eat bread till you return to the ground. For out of it you were taken; for dust you are, and to dust you shall return."

Some might say that's a pretty harsh punishment. Upon your first read-through, you might think that God hates them. Then to add insult to injury, He kicks them out the garden. God seems like He is furious. Yet, the next thing He does shows that He truly loves Adam and Eve. Genesis 3:21 states that for Adam and Eve, "God made tunics of skin, and clothed them." So put this in perspective. You and your biological father have a great relationship, always spending quality time together. Then one day he kicks you out his house for breaking his rules. Even if he doesn't want to, he holds true to his punishment. Before he puts you out though, he gives you $500 out his wallet to help you on your journey. You might not understand his rationale, but you can't deny that he cares about your well-being outside of the situation. God loved Adam and Eve, but they were disobedient. The enemy knew how righteous God was, and still is today. Satan also knew that God couldn't lie, and would have to go through with a punishment. God did just that, but afterward, he preciously clothed them. They were still His kids, good or bad. We have to acknowledge that after the sin, He still loved and walked with them.

To cement this, all we have to do is read Genesis 4:15. When Cain killed his brother Abel, God cursed him. Cain cried out to God that his punishment was too much for him to bear. He felt that he would be hidden from the face of God. The Lord replied, "Therefore whoever kills Cain, vengeance shall be taken on him sevenfold." God was still in contact with Adam and Eve's family. Cain, Adam's son, killed his own brother, but God still protected him after the curse. So both of these examples show that God's laws are His laws. He will enforce what He says. Those laws, though, are separate from his love. Those laws were put in place because of His love, but they don't dictate his love. He loved Cain, even after he killed Abel. If He didn't, He wouldn't have spoken a holy word of protection around Cain.

So think about that and let's go back to the reprimand that God gave to Adam. The curse that God said wasn't directed at man, but it would be turmoil to the man. Man will have to work to eat, and the ground by which he will till, will bring forth thorns and thistles. This job will not be an easy day's work. You and I today still have to work jobs to earn a check. That check provides us a paper of monetary value that allows us to buy food to eat, and many other things. We can't get away from working. You have to earn your keep in this world, and you know that. How then do you prosper? You have to work. The curse on the ground made Adam have to work to prosper, but God was still with him. He blessed his work. You have to know this so you can get in agreement with God and His will for you. Many of you are barely making ends meet with your jobs, and have been asking God to give you a financial breakthrough. Due to what He spoke to Adam, we have to work, but God will bless the increase.

Now when I say work, I'm not specifically speaking about a job. God might be asking that same person who needs the breakthrough to donate his or her time at the Boys and Girls Club. The Holy Spirit speaks to you every time you pass the building, but you refuse because you have to go home and figure out a way to get the money. If you were to listen to the Holy Spirit, your blessing might be attached to someone in the building. You could do a great job mentoring a child, to find out later that the child's parents own their own company. Instead of giving you a job to increase your finances, they show you how to start your own company. You would not have been in this situation sitting at home in a prayer closet for a week straight. God knows that you have to work. He commanded it of us. I was praying for an increase in my finances, and He told me to write this book. He didn't just give me money; He gave me a task to work and complete. All He told me was that He would bless my work and answer my prayer. I still had to give my own efforts to complete it.

We have to work and God will bless it. Your goal should be to ask God to show you what it is you should be working on. Sometimes it's not even the thing that will bring the financial gain. Sometimes He has to prepare us before we can get to that point of responsibility. God won't give you something you're not ready for that can potentially harm you. Would you give your child a loaded gun just because he requested it? HECK NO! Would you prepare your child about the dangers that surround him when using a loaded gun? ABSOLUTELY! Afterward, you might take him out to shoot where he can be properly educated. As the child matures in his training, he'll be able to handle those dangers. Many of us are so frustrated at God. We are blessed with a job, but we complain, thinking we are above our position. We lose our thankfulness and begin to curse the gift God gives us. How do you know that your breakthrough isn't attached to where you are right now? God won't give you $1,000,000 just to watch you lose your faith, your life, and everything in between. He's the ultimate Father. He knows what His kids can handle. He doesn't tell us no, just not right now. He prepares us for our blessings. The thing is, the way He teaches us isn't always conventional.

I've seen people pray to God asking for financial gain, and He would respond by telling them to give their lasts to a specific person or group in need. Some responded with, "What? I only have ten dollars to my name God and you want me to give it to someone else? That's why I'm praying for more money!" They don't know that God is about to supernaturally bless them with not just a little money, but an abundance of finances. He just wants them to line up the desires of their hearts with His word. Out of their mouths, they might say they will do right by the money, but God sees their hearts. He knows that they might brag about their blessing, or blow it because they don't manage money properly. He continues to send people to help them stay afloat financially, but He is waiting on their acceptance of the lessons before He can open up the flood gate. That way He knows you are more than able to do what He requires of you when you receive His blessing.

God doesn't want you to go backward, so he'll prepare your heart to do right by His blessing the first time. You still have to listen to the Holy Spirit and follow His direction. So if you are praying for your breakthrough and haven't received it, ask God what you need to work on to get it right. We must think and speak in agreement with God. He knows you, so you need to get to know Him. If anybody really has a relationship with the Lord, they'll tell you that God desires your intimacy. Before you get your breakthrough, He wants you to talk to Him and know His voice. He wants you to include Him in your decision-making process. Stop making your own decisions, falling in a hole, then asking God to get you out. You have to walk with Him to get His blessing. We have to renew our minds.

What is your normal mind when your mind is renewed?

A renewed mind is being able to keep your thoughts focused on God and His greatness. When Saul was converted on the road to Damascus, Jesus renewed his mind. He still was the same man as before, but his mind was different. He didn't try to change because the church told him to change. He was transformed because he heard the truth for himself. He knew it would be outright dumb to trade that truth for a lie. He was able to focus because he trusted his revelation. In Galatians 1:11-16, Paul's Epistle to the Galatians describes his conversion as a divine revelation. He writes,

> But I make known to you, brethren, that the gospel which was preached by me is not according to man. For I neither received it from man, nor was I taught it, but it came through the revelation of Jesus Christ. For you have heard of my former conduct in Judaism, how I persecuted the church of God beyond measure and tried to destroy it. And I advanced in Judaism beyond many of my contemporaries in my own nation, being more exceedingly zealous for the traditions of my fathers. But when it pleased God, who separated me from my mother's womb and

> called me through His grace, to reveal His
> Son in me, that I might preach Him among
> the Gentiles, I did not immediately confer
> with flesh and blood.

Paul said that when God called him, through His grace, he did not immediately consult any human being. He didn't force his mind into a state of renewal; the truth renewed his mind. Once God reveals himself to you, there is no denying the truth. It's one thing to speculate that your boyfriend is cheating on you, but when the truth is revealed to you, how can you keep on as if nothing happened? How can you go back to your old way of living while holding onto this vital information? Once you are presented with the truth, your perspective changes. You might not leave your boyfriend, but that variable does shift the dynamic of the relationship. God wants to reveal His true self to you. I'm not talking about the idea of God, but the TRUE LIVING GOD! Jesus spoke to a group of Jews in John 8:31-32, "If you abide in My word, you are My disciples indeed. And you shall know the truth, and the truth shall make you free." That freedom is the basis of your mind renewal. That freedom is also derived from you knowing the truth about Jesus and His teachings. Just like Saul's conversion, you won't be the same. God will continue to give you more revelations through the Holy Spirit, so that you can have a better understanding of Him. Again I say, ultimately all God wants is intimacy with His children. He is the best parent in the world...literally!

He wants us to renew our minds so that we can operate in His realm instead of in the world's. For example, let's say you are an actor. You've been working really hard on your craft, and praying through it all. You've gone to audition after audition. Late one night, you get a phone call. It's the casting director for a major motion picture. She says they came across your demo reel, and the director specifically wants you to audition in two days for the main role. You hang up, filled with joy. All that hard work has finally caught up to you. This could be the opportunity that changes your life. You call all your family and friends to share the good news. After you're done, the enemy speaks to you. "This is a big step. You might embarrass yourself. Not only will you not get the part, but you will make such an ass of yourself that they will clown you throughout the industry. You will be known by this horrendous performance." At that very moment, what would you do? Really ask yourself. Most people, including me, would start freaking out and rehearsing their lines over and over again. You already know the lines backward and forward, but you are focused on the lie. How many of us would have opened our bibles and read Philippians 4:6-7? Paul wrote, "Be anxious for nothing, but in everything by prayer and supplication, with thanksgiving, let your requests be made known to God; and the peace of God, which sur-passes all understanding, will guard your hearts and minds through Christ Jesus." Could you have read that scripture and sustained yourself for the duration of your audition?

How many of us would have had the tenacity of David when he fought Goliath? God's will is for you to trust in Him. God doesn't want you to stress. Stress is a worldly mindset. People who lack the knowledge about the power of God, Jesus Christ, and the Holy Spirit stress when the odds are against them. In 1 Samuel 17:45-47, David went up to Goliath and told him,

> You come to me with a sword, with a spear, and with a javelin. But I come to you in the name of the Lord of hosts, the God of the armies of Israel, whom you have defied. This day the Lord will deliver you into my hand, and I will strike you and take your head from you. And this day I will give the carcasses

of the camp of the Philistines to the birds of
the air and the wild beasts of the earth, that
all the earth may know that there is a God in
Israel. Then all this assembly shall know that
the Lord does not save with sword and spear,
for the battle is the Lord's, and He will give
you into our hands.

He spoke that while standing in front of the Philistine
army and his own people. What a bold declaration of faith.
When David spoke about "the Lord does not save with sword
and spear, for the battle is the Lord's, and He will give you
into our hands," that's mind renewal. He didn't focus on the
imminent chance of death. He stood on the promises of God
the entire time.

You can only stand up in the middle of the storm if you
have God-given revelation. If you just speak the Word of
God, but don't truly have a relationship with the Father, when
times get hard you will run. You will miss your moment of
revelation because you can't shift your focus to the revealer.
Ask the three Hebrew boys, Shadrach, Meshach, and Abed-
Nego. In Daniel 3:13-18, King Nebuchadnezzar was angry
because these gentlemen wouldn't bow before the golden
image. The scriptures read,

> Then Nebuchadnezzar, in rage and fury,
> gave the command to bring Shadrach,
> Meshach and Abed-Nego. So they brought
> these men before the king. Nebuchadnezzar
> spoke saying, to them, "Is it true, Shadrach,
> Meshach and Abed-Nego, that you do not
> serve my gods or worship the gold image
> which I have set up? Now if you are ready
> at the time you hear the sound of the horn,
> flute, harp, lyre, and psaltery, in symphony

with all kinds of music, and you fall down and worship the image which I have made, good! But if you do not worship, you shall be cast immediately into the midst of a burning fiery furnace. And who is the god who will deliver you from my hands?" Shadrach, Meshach and Abed-Nego answered and said to the king, "O Nebuchadnezzar, we have no need to answer you in this matter. If that is the case, our God whom we serve is able to deliver us from the burning fiery furnace, and He will deliver us from your hand, O king. But if not, let it be known to you, O king, that we do not serve your gods, nor will we worship the gold image which you have set up."

That's the renewing of your mind. You don't do things because the world does them. You stand up for WHO you believe in.

Along this war path of mind renewal, you will have battle scars. Satan doesn't want you to renew ANYTHING, not even a DVD rental. He will try to intimidate you through others. He will speak a word in them if he can't get to you. He will attack you at all costs because he knows once you see the truth, you will stay in its power. At times, you might give in and bow down to your own representation of the golden image. God is not condemning you for that. Instead, He is sending His word in various forms to usher you to a renewed state; hence you reading this book right now. God wants all of us to be molded to where we are strong enough, in the Spirit, to withstand the temptations. Don't beat yourself up when trying to put on your "garment of righteousness." It takes time to change clothes. We are surrounded by thoughts of negativity as soon as we are born. Many were brought up in a household that didn't speak the promises of God.

Instead, they spoke the "what ifs." "What if you die?" "What if you don't succeed?" "What if it doesn't work?" "What if?" "What if?" "What if…blah, blah, blah, blah, blah." God said, "Renew you mind by focusing on the truth." The truth is the Word of God. Trust the revelations given to you by the Holy Spirit, and enjoy the freedom that people outside the covering of Christ don't understand. That renewal will also bring people to the faith. They will see how God exalts you through the good and the bad. They will see how you stand on the Word of God, even when something terrible happens. They will know that ONLY God could have changed you. This renewal brings peace and direction to your life. This renewal allows you to cast ALL of your cares upon our precious Lord and Savior, Jesus Christ.

Understand that your mind aids your spirit.

God wants to use you, but your mind is too busy. When I was younger, I would worry up a storm. I would go to my mom with all this stress, and she would tell me to talk to God about it. I would whine, saying that I did, but I didn't know if He responded. Then I would blame Him, saying that He is confusing me. She would sternly say back that, "God is not a God of confusion." In Matthew 7:9-11, Jesus said, "Or what man is there among you who, if his son asks for bread, will give him a stone? Or if he asks for a fish, will he give him a serpent? If you then, being evil, know how to give good gifts to your children, how much more will your Father who is in heaven give good things to those who ask Him!" So why would God give me, His child, a spirit of confusion? She knew I was blaming God for the attacks of Satan. My mom would tell me that God is faithful, and that He will respond. She said I just have to look for the answer and be prepared for what that answer is, whether I hate it or love it. The thing is though, the devil makes it so hard to concentrate on that answer. When we partially hear God's voice, we tend to fill in the lost words. Then God's clear message gets cluttered. Going back to the point noted earlier, God is not a God of confusion. If I understand this, then I will really seek God during these times. Instead, we allow the mind to wander and do whatever it wants to do, which the devil loves. He will constantly speak numerous scenarios to your mind, knowing that all of them lead to death and destruction.

You might say, "C.J., that's a little over-the-top," but is it really? We stress all day over every important and minute thing. Some have grown spiritually to where Satan can fool them, but he can't keep them in the rabbit hole. Once they see his plot, they allow God to deliver them from the circumstances. Since he can't keep them paralyzed under his lies, the enemy will just continue to speak the lies to confuse them. That doubt will take its own course. The devil knows that as long as you don't know the voice of God clearly, you will just listen to ANY voice. Then you become the kid that walks up to a car window because the driver offers you a piece of candy. We know what happens to those poor kids. These are tricks from the enemy. If he can keep you in a state of confusion, your mind and your physical body will continue to wander aimlessly through life. Then you think that your lack of success from your decisions is God's fault. The enemy comes right behind you speaking, "God isn't real. You're just speaking to the air while ALL these people around you are climbing above you. They don't care what they did to get their success, why should you?" "You're going to be poor, and an idiot because you called out to God for help, and He didn't come!"

This is another time that you should capture your thoughts to aid your spirit. These thoughts have yet to become actions. Right then, we should lean on the words that God promised us a "covenant relationship." Our mental state is out of control, and this is our time to kneel at Jesus' feet with our worries. Instead, many decide to self-medicate. That self-medication isn't always hard drugs and alcohol. Some people self-medicate by separating from their families, over-eating, being hurtful to others, blowing their money, becoming workaholics, mentally attacking themselves with their own hurtful words, etc. You become depressed, and then separation occurs. You think that separation was your own idea, but the enemy isolates you. When you are really depressed, it affects your body. You stop doing the daily tasks needed to keep up your temple. Sometimes you don't even feel like showering or eating. You become extremely fatigued, allowing Satan to attack your mind and body with diseases and other things. The reason is because your weakened state, in the physical realm, makes it easier to accept defeat in the spiritual realm. Any other time, if a feeling of depression came over you, you might say, "I'm not gonna let that get me down," and walk right out of it. When you are in the state of depression, you start to accept and dwell on thoughts that normally you would dismiss. The thoughts have always been there because the devil doesn't take days off. This time, though, we ate the pudding.

Finally, we have fallen into a pit of darkness. We try to comprehend what's going on around us, but to no avail. The only thing that can save us from drowning in the sea of lies and deception is the Holy Truth. That's why Proverbs 4:20-27 is so powerful. It reads,

> My son, give attention to my words; Incline your ear to my sayings. Do not let them depart from your eyes; Keep them in the midst of your heart; For they are life to those who find them, and health to all their flesh. Keep your heart with all diligence, for out of it spring the issues of life. Put away from you a deceitful mouth, and put perverse lips far from you.

> Let your eyes look straight ahead, and your
> eyelids look right before you. Ponder the path
> at your feet, and let all your ways be estab-
> lished. Do not turn to the right or the left;
> remove your foot from evil.

God demands constancy of the heart. He knows walking this path of wisdom is not a casual thing. He understands your mind aids your spirit; therefore, He gives us clear instructions on how to cultivate both. We have to forcefully keep our thoughts on our almighty Creator, never moving left or right until we heed His voice. This will require discipline.

God is ALWAYS in the business of teaching principles of discipline.

We can't properly work out of the will of God unless we are disciplined. It takes dedication to deny your body of its fleshly desires. The wall of self-restraint is being built throughout your life. Every brick, neatly placed or aggressively removed, is crafted from our decisions. Before you can grasp the full understanding of being disciplined, you have to understand why there is a need to be disciplined. Proverbs 25:28 says, "Whoever has no rule over his own spirit is like a city broken down, without walls." Self-control is a critical part of obedience to God. Without it, like the city broken down and without walls, we are open to attacks. We lose the pride and respect for the space occupied by God's precious Holy Spirit, which is our temple.

Galatians 5:22-23 says, "But the fruit of the Spirit is love, joy, peace, long-suffering, kindness, goodness, faithfulness, gentleness, self-control. Against such there is no law." We are spiritually "crucified" with Jesus, therefore, we no longer have to follow the values or desires of the world. However, we know how hard it is to apply this spiritual truth to our passionate affections and desires of the flesh. It's a constant struggle to master our sinful appetite. Those who enjoy success focused on God. In the book of Jeremiah, he is speaking to the only Jewish nation left, Judah. God instructed Jeremiah to speak to them a message of doom that was approaching fast. That doom included invasion and annihilation, ending in exile of the people from their land. Along with this message, hope was attached. He was also told to deliver the news that God would restore the nation. The Jews would get a second chance if they got back to true kingdom business. God wanted their focus, and would go through great lengths to make sure His children were disciplined. Jeremiah spoke to the Jews in Jeremiah 9:23-24, "Thus says the Lord: 'Let not the wise man glory in his wisdom, Let not the mighty man glory in his might, Nor let the rich man glory in his riches; But let him who glories glory in this, That he understands and knows Me, That I am the Lord, exercising loving-kindness, judgment, and righteousness in the earth. For in these I delight,' says the Lord."

The individuals that Jeremiah was speaking to were leaning on their own capabilities rather than focusing on God. He wanted them to find their true worth in knowing the Living God, honoring Him for His glorious virtue. They preferred to praise themselves and their own efforts. God had to discipline them before He could bring them into their glory. Since you have a basis for why we are disciplined, let's look at what it means to be disciplined in a biblical sense. In the book of Galatians, Paul encouraged the Galatians to walk in the Spirit because they were already living in the Spirit. One would think that connection would be natural, but remember, we are at war with the enemy and our own flesh. Paul didn't give them a way, based upon their own merit, to change their outcomes in life. He told them bluntly in Galatians 5:25, "If we live in the Spirit, let us also walk in the Spirit." Walking in the Spirit means to listen and be obedient to the prompting of the Holy Spirit. God knows that a believer following the lead of the Holy Spirit will not fall short. He sent Him to us, as our Helper, for this very reason. God knows we aren't able to be nor remain holy on our own. He trains us to capture every thought and put it up against the Word of God. When we refuse to do so, we are convicted by the Holy Spirit to repent and get it right. That's all part of God's discipline.

Hebrews 12:11 reads, "Now no chastening seems to be joyful for the present, but painful; nevertheless, afterward it yields the peaceable fruit of righteousness to those who have been trained by it." Learning how to be disciplined in your life is not always pretty, but it's always necessary. That principle is true to a believer and non-believer alike. God knows that the more He teaches you discipline, the more you will realize that Satan is no longer in control of your actions. You now take control over your thoughts, which brings life, because you know God is always in control of your life. Now God can help you grow in your faith because of you openly accepting His discipline.

One Corinthians 10:13 says, "No temptation has over-taken you except such as common to man; but God is faithful, who will not allow you to be tempted beyond what you are able, but with the temptation will also make the way of escape, that you may be able to bear it." You being trained in self-discipline allows God to place you in certain environments, safe and unsafe, so that He can be exalted among the people. If I had been put in jail when I was in my early twenties, I probably would have earned several more charges. I know, without a doubt, I would have run the jail. Anything about Jesus would have been in the back of my mind, the very back. At that age, I lacked God's self-discipline. When I did get locked up in my late twenties, God and I already had a relationship. I wasn't always listening to the Holy Spirit, but He was definitely correcting my thoughts.

While incarcerated, I was still able to be used for the kingdom of God. He gave me opportunities to be real with some of the other inmates. I gave my testimonies about God, prayed with people, had bible study with some during our break time, etc. Old C.J. would have just focused on the fact that he didn't deserve to be in jail. Even though the circumstances should have been in my favor to not get locked up, I did. That's that. I knew God had me, so I played the hand I was dealt. I just focused on God, like I try to do every day. My present situation didn't change my daily communion with God. Because I was able to seek His guidance during this tough time, God granted me staying power through those same tough times. Due to me adhering to His discipline, He was able to use me to fight against Satan's lies by spreading truth.

God will send His shepherds all over to get His flock, even when those people don't acknowledge that they are part of His flock. In Matthew 18:12-14, Jesus said, "What do you think? If a man has a hundred sheep, and one of them goes astray, does he not leave the ninety-nine and go to the mountains to seek the one that is straying? And if he should find it, assuredly, I say to you, he rejoices more over that sheep than over the ninety-nine that did not go astray. Even so it is not the will of your Father who is in heaven that one of these little ones should perish." God has to discipline us so that He can use us effectively. He wants intimacy with ALL of his children. Some of those children are in places that most of us don't want to go. Nobody wants to be sent by God to minister inside a jail, or go to a hostile country in war and speak the love of Jesus Christ. Most Christians, who speak a good game about their belief in what the Father can do, will move from a neighborhood because of gangs before praying to see what they can do to help these gang members find Jesus Christ and receive salvation.

You have to be disciplined by the Holy Spirit to be able to be used in supernatural situations. That is because God is going to ask of you things that are not normal. If you aren't trained to hear the voice of the Lord, and know His ways and teachings, you will crumble under pressure. The enemy is too cunning and the flesh is too weak. I guarantee you will fail if you depend on your own strength. Faith is built upon discipline. You learn to have faith in the Lord because He shows up during your trials. Your trials give Him an opportunity to teach you through the Holy Spirit. The Holy Spirit teaches you the true voice of God. That voice leads you to victory, no matter the battle. That is the reason why God disciplines us. He knows His voice isn't the only voice that you will hear. Because you have free will, you have to choose to whom you want to listen. When you learn to hear God's voice through your tribulations, you will start to see that trials aren't a negative thing. How can anything be negative when you know God is in control, and it will work out in the end for our good? That end is to include death.

The book of Hebrews eloquently speaks on this subject. I will just recite a few sections so that I can bring the point home. Hebrews 11:17-19 says, "By faith Abraham, when he was tested, offered up Isaac, and he who had received the promises offered up his only begotten son, of whom it was said, 'In Isaac your seed shall be called,' concluding that God was able to raise him up, even from the dead, from which he also received him in a figurative sense." When Abraham was tested, he believed that God could raise Isaac from the dead. Even though he didn't want to kill his son, He had to be disciplined to listen to the voice of God and follow through with the command that God gave him.

Hebrews 11:24-26 reads, "By faith Moses, when he became of age, refused to be called the son of Pharaoh's daughter, choosing rather to suffer affliction with the people of God than to enjoy the passing pleasures of sin, esteeming the reproach of Christ greater riches than the treasures in Egypt; for he looked to the reward." Moses believed in God, and refused a high position in Pharaohs' court. He, instead,

chose to suffer with his people. He had to be disciplined
to know God's voice and choose His promise over all the
worldly luxuries that were before him. That discipline provided a way for God to show His mercy, by allowing Moses
to take His people out of slavery in Egypt. That discipline
also allowed him to hear God's voice and implement the
Passover, which we still celebrate.

How many of you would quit a job that pays you mil-
lions of corrupt dollars, and live on the streets? Would you
quit, if that same company you worked for was taking homeless people off the streets and making them their slaves? It's
one thing to say you would when you are broke. It's another
thing to say you would, while lying in your million dollar
bed located in the west wing of your GIGANTIC mansion.
At that moment, would you let all of that go for the right
reason? That's something to think about. I feel that Hebrews
11:30-40 sums this principle up properly:

> By faith the walls of Jericho fell down after
> they were encircled for seven days. By faith
> the harlot Rahab did not perish with those
> who did not believe, when she had received
> the spies with peace. And what more shall
> I say? For the time would fail me to tell of
> Gideon and Barak and Samson and Jephthah,
> also of David and Samuel and the prophets:
> who through faith subdued kingdoms, worked
> righteousness, obtained promises, stopped
> the mouths of lions, quenched the violence
> of fire, escaped the edge of the sword, out
> of weakness were made strong, became val-
> iant in battle, turned to fight the armies of the
> aliens. Women received their dead raised to
> life again. Others were tortured, not accepting
> deliverance, that they might obtain a better

resurrection. Still others had trial of mocking and scourging, yes, and of chains and imprisonment. They were stoned, they were sawn in two, were tempted, were slain with the sword. They wandered about in sheepskins and goatskins, being destitute, afflicted, tormented-of whom the world was not worthy. They wandered in deserts and mountains, in dens and caves of the earth. And all these, having obtained a good testimony through faith, did not receive the promise, God having provided something better for us, that they should not be made perfect apart from us.

It took faith for the warriors of Israel to destroy the walled city of Jericho by such an unconventional manner. Yet, their act of faith and discipline to follow God's directions precisely gave them the desired result. The scripture also notes that not all who had faith won victories during their hour of faith. Many were tortured and killed. Their deaths still had a purpose in the great scheme of God's plan. If it weren't so, we wouldn't still be debating about people and experiences written in the bible. Those events still impact our lives today. Many of these people got to see God's glory in their own lives because they were disciplined in their faith. That discipline just comes from being in a relationship with the Lord. The Holy Spirit will do the rest over time. Believe that!

We have to practice taking action and making ourselves aware of the problems.

Many times we lack discipline because we tend to place our faults on others. We can't gain self-control in any areas if we never acknowledge that we need the discipline. We have to begin with taking ownership of who we are, and where we are at this time in our lives. Two Timothy 2:21 says, "Therefore if anyone cleanses himself from the latter, he will be a vessel for honor, sanctified and useful for the Master, prepared for every good work." A fighter, like Mike Tyson, doesn't just wake up one day and say, "Tomorrow I want to fight the heavy weight champion." What I can see him saying is, "Tomorrow I will start training, and soon I will be prepared to fight the heavy weight champion." To get to tomorrow, we have to deal with today. God wants to bless your future, but we have to confess our past and accept our present. Confessing acknowledges the elephant in the room, and it will free you from the physical feeling of condemnation that's spiritually attached to the sin.

Let me give you an example to help clarify. How many times have you committed a sin, and minutes later regretted the action? You might have cheated on your spouse, cursed out your parents, stole something from work, etc. When you don't speak about what you have done, doesn't it feel like you're carrying a weight around? I don't mean this just in a symbolic sense. I feel a physical weight that lays heavy on me. That weight then begins to affect things that are physically separate from the situation. Things like my job or my relationships may start to suffer. That's why the bible speaks heavily on confessing your sins, to God and to one another. One John 1:7-10 states, "But if we walk in the light as He is in the light, we have fellowship with one another, and the blood of Jesus Christ His Son cleanses us from all sin. If we say that we have no sin, we deceive ourselves, and the truth is not in us. If we confess our sins, He is faithful and just to forgive us our sins and to cleanse us from all unrighteousness. If we say we have not sinned, we make Him a liar, and His word is not in us." The light is God's truth. What is God's truth? That truth is "the blood of Jesus Christ His Son [that] cleanses us from all sin." We aren't confessing our sins to God to gain salvation; Jesus died for that already.

We confess our sins to God for the same reason your parents made you confess your wrongdoings. You have to acknowledge that something's wrong before you can head back toward what's right. Confessing our sins to the Lord opens us to accepting His discipline.

Believers will not suffer eternal damnation for our sins, but we often still suffer daily consequences. Your child leaves the house, after you told him not to, so you decide to punish him. When he comes home, he walks around like nothing happened. This creates a certain awkwardness in the room. You bring up what he did, and he still denies his wrongdoing. This divides both of you and hinders the fellowship within your relationship. With God, it is the same way. Our lack of admitting our sin hinders our commune with God. You begin to run from His presence like Adam and Eve in the Garden of Eden. The devil knows that, and will try to keep you away from God. That's the enemy's way of keeping the weight on you. He knows that once you confess what you did, you let it go. He wants you to get numb to the sin. Satan wants you to think that you don't have to confess anything to God. As long as you keep it to yourself, you're golden.

To be honest, it's really hard sometimes to confess your sin to people around you. At times, that confession brings judgment. People will gossip all day about what you're doing, only because what they are doing hasn't made the headlines yet. So why would the Word of God say that we should confess our sins to Him and to one another? James 5:16 reads, "Confess your trespasses to one another, and pray for one another, that you may be healed. The effective, fervent prayer of a righteous man avails much." Confessing our sins to each other shows our weakness and the need for God to be in our lives. If everybody was real about the sins they commit daily, more people would come and get to know Jesus. We would all realize that EVERYBODY is messed up. We all have vices and demons we are fighting. It's crazy how I hear people talk about ministers on television, like T.D. Jakes or Joel Osteen, as if they don't sin. I remember being in a conversation with some of my church members, and I said, "You know T.D. Jakes *could* be at home watching porn right now." The entire room froze. They all hit me with a look of disgust. I wasn't trying to hate on T.D. Jakes. I don't know him, but he seems like a good guy. I was just making the point that he does something sinful every day. We all do. We aren't different from one another. We are all going through life. We need to pray for one another against the attacks from the enemy. How can I get you to pray for me in a particular area if I can't share my sin with you? As the body of Christ, we have to get pass our personal judgment zones toward others. They're all traps from the enemy.

In John, chapter four, Jesus goes to the region of Samaria. He sits by a well and has a conversation with a Samaritan woman. He asks her for a drink. Remember, during these times, Jews really didn't talk to Samaritans. The Jews taught that the Samaritans were ritually unclean. By her giving Jesus some of her water, that was supposed to make Him unclean. She responds in John 4:9, "How is it that You, being a Jew, ask a drink from me, a Samaritan woman? For Jews have no dealings with Samaritans." Jesus answers back, "If you knew the gift of God, and who it is who says to you, 'Give Me a drink,' you would have asked Him, and He would have given you living water." Later in the conversation, she becomes curious about this "living water" that Jesus says will spring up into everlasting life. She requests the water, and Jesus says to her, "Go, call your husband and come here." She replies, "I have no husband." Then Jesus shows her His power. He replies, "You have well said, 'I have no husband,' for you have five husbands, and the one whom you now have is not your husband; in that you spoke truly." Jesus knew she had been married, and that she was shacking up with a guy right then. Jesus didn't judge her. He didn't point his finger and say, "May the wrath of God devour you right now!" He just wanted her to acknowledge her sin. He knew that she had to own her sin, so that she could see the need to partake in His everlasting water that He spoke about. His main goal was her salvation. Jesus knew that if she received eternal life, she wouldn't be the same. She might feel the same, but spiritually, a change would have taken place. That's just the spiritual order of things. You have to let it take its course.

The enemy knows that there are laws in place that govern the spiritual realm. God shares them with us, but we have to follow through. For instance, in Matthew 18:19-20, Jesus specifically says, "Again I say to you that if two of you agree on earth concerning anything that they ask, it will be done for them by My Father in heaven. For where two or three are gathered together in My name, I am there in the midst of them." That's straight from the mouth of Jesus. So why do you think the devil wants you to close off your short-comings to others, and gossip when you hear people reveal their sin? He knows that it will cause separation. He knows it will cause division by order of ranks. Certain people will put themselves on a spiritual high horse and talk down to others. The enemy also knows that if it were done right, we as the church would be too powerful to handle. Think about it. If we all were open about who we are, then popes and ministers wouldn't be treated as God. They would be treated as men of God, mortal men, may I add. Christians wouldn't walk around like they know a secret that was only given to them. We would always just talk about how great God is because of how weak we are.

We are all being beat up by Satan, let's face it. It's rough out here trying to follow the guidance of the Holy Spirit. We need each other and our prayers. Prayer does work, so prayer in numbers especially works. That's a spiritual law that the devil keeps you from utilizing. We can't speak badly about someone, then pray for him or her ten minutes later.

Do you think God takes that prayer seriously? Would you if you were Him? How can you expect your words to be heartfelt, when ten minutes prior you just spoke poorly about that same person you're praying for? Again, that is why we confess our sins: to get back in the will of God. Confession keeps open our connection. By admitting we are sinners, it makes grace that much more of an impactful gift. I get so excited when I think about how much God loves me, even when I can't say it back to Him.

Romans 3:23 says, "For all have sinned and fall short of the glory of God." Grace from the Father is free. Jesus died for your sins. So in that regard, as long as you believe in Jesus as your Lord and personal Savior, you're forgiven. Like any parent molding a child, you won't like all of His rules. You will venture off and do your own thing at times, but God will change a willing heart. He knows His children from the fakes. God doesn't need me to go tell you if your relationship isn't true. He's all-knowing. So your best bet is to quit playing Him like He's stupid. God knows your heart, so just be real and confess what it is.

I know this is a lot to take in, just don't let unbelief and doubt steal your peace.

As believers, we can enter into rest with God. Unbelief refers to one who habitually or instinctively doubts or questions. Like I said before, we have to practice taking action and making ourselves aware of the problems. The mark we should set as Christians is to grow and be more like Christ every day. It takes faith to take on this daunting task. When Moses spoke to the Israelites in Deuteronomy, he told them, "I call heaven and earth as witnesses today against you, that I have set before you life and death, blessing and cursing; therefore choose life, that both you and your descendants may live; that you may love the Lord your God, that you may obey His voice, and that you may cling to Him, for He is your life and the length of your days; and that you may dwell in the land which the Lord swore to your fathers, to Abraham, Isaac, and Jacob, to give them." Placed before you is life and death. You have to make your own decisions. God will prompt you to which decision will better suit you, but you still have to make the decision.

When Jesus was being tempted in the wilderness by the enemy, He could have cried out that God had left Him. He could have said, "Father forgive me, for this burden is too heavy," followed by Him giving in to the devil. Jesus held strong to what He believed. He didn't let doubt or unbelief creep in. He stood on the same belief, in the same God, as when He was doing great feats. When He was healing people, God was real. So when He was going through His trial, God had to still be real. Nothing changed but His circumstance.

We always call on the name of God when positive things occur in our lives, but as soon as the current gets rough, we want to survive by our own life preserver. We start to doubt the voice of God, preferring to focus on our own desires and fears. We say we have faith, but we sometimes have a weird way of showing it. That time of turmoil is the buildup in the movie before you get to the great ending. You can't truly appreciate warmth without being extremely cold. You need some gloom to see God's glory. That's how He combats your disbelief in the supernatural. He will show up, but in a way that you can't deny it was Him. But after a while, God wants to show you more. He can't spend half of your life just doing parlor tricks so that you can stay on His team. He wants to ride with you beyond the training wheels. The only way He can accomplish that is to place you in situations so that He can refine you. In those situations, He can get your attention. He can show you His power. He can bless you beyond measure. He can establish a genuine relationship with you. After all that, all He wants you to do is trust Him. Come under His care. He doesn't want you to worry, just be ready!

Worrying hinders our progress. God already told us that He will provide; what more do we need? Matthew 6:25-34 states,

> Therefore I say to you, do not worry about your life, what you will eat or what you will drink; nor about your body, what you will put on. Is not life more than food and the body more than clothing? Look at the birds of the air, for they neither sow nor reap nor gather into barns; yet your heavenly Father feeds them. Are you not of more value than they? Which of you by worrying can add one cubit to his stature? So why do you worry about clothing? Consider the lilies of the field, how they grow: they neither toil nor spin; and yet I say to you that even Solomon in all his glory was not arrayed like one of these. Now if God so clothes the grass of the field, which today is, and tomorrow is thrown into the oven, will He not much more clothe you, O you of little faith? Therefore do not worry, saying, "What shall we eat?" or "What shall we drink?" or "What shall we wear?" For after all these things the Gentiles seek. For your heavenly Father knows that you need all these things. But seek first the kingdom of God and His righteousness, and all these things shall be added to you. Therefore do not worry about tomorrow, for tomorrow will worry about its own things. Sufficient for the day is its own trouble.

Why embark on such a race that never brings success at the finish line? Nobody ever gained anything besides grey hairs from stressing. The situation you have played over and over again in your imagination is going to play out in its own, natural way. You worrying won't change the outcome.

What if some of the key people in stories documented in the bible worried instead of going through? What about the women in Luke, chapter eight, with the issue of blood? The bible says in Luke 8:43-44 that, "a woman, having a flow of blood for twelve years, who had spent all her livelihood on physicians and could not be healed by any, came from behind and touched the border of His [Jesus'] garment. And immediately her flow of blood stopped." Jesus was surrounded by people. She could have sat there worrying about things like, "What if this doesn't work?" "What if the people from the crowd think I'm crazy for doing this?" "I've been trying to get medically healed for years. I'm just destined to be sick." She could have rationalized all of these things and never touched Jesus' garment. Then she probably would have cursed God, thinking He didn't love her. She did none of these things. She didn't cripple herself by worrying beyond what she could handle. She let go and let God handle the situation. All she was able to do was touch His garment, so she did just that. She let the outcome be the outcome.

What about in Mark, chapter seven, when Jesus healed a deaf man with poor speech? Jesus was going to the Sea of Galilee, and a multitude brought Him to the deaf gentleman. Jesus had shown in earlier events that He could just touch a person, and they would be healed. This time however, He chose a more unorthodox way to perform the miracle. The way Jesus went about it, the deaf guy had to have faith in His power. Jesus put His fingers in the deaf guy's ears, and He spat and touched his tongue. Then, looking up to heaven, He sighed, and said to him, "Ephphatha," that is, "Be opened." Immediately his ears were opened, the impediment of his tongue was loosed, and he spoke plainly. What if you went to the hospital because of the same issue, and your doctor dug in your ear with his finger? Some might be creeped out, others might go with it. Then after that, he tells you to open your mouth so that he can touch your tongue, with his dirty finger. That makes thoughts run rampant in my brain. He could have told Jesus, "I'm sick, sir, but this is just plain disgusting." He could have worried about the idea of diseases to the point where he denied Jesus' help. What did he do though? He just sought his healing. He believed, and therefore received. He didn't worry about the ridicule from others. To be totally honest, he was probably ridiculed throughout his life for being disabled. I'm sure people back in those times weren't any less rude than people nowadays.

Some of you are waiting on your blessing or healing, and God is asking you to trust Him. He hasn't given you a spirit of worry, but you receive it from the enemy. You start to question the process, instead of just receiving your blessing from the process. Somebody reading this has quit their job. You know you need the income, and you've been praying to God for a way out of the situation. He has told you several times to humble yourself and go ask for your job back. You know you hear the voice of God, but you are worrying about external factors. You know people at your job saw what happened. You're nervous because you know they will talk about you. You don't want to seem weak to them. You don't know how it's going to be, after the previous incident that led to you quitting. Go get what you have been desiring of God. Trust that He has worked out that situation before you even return. Once you go back, you will remember what you have read, and it will anchor your faith in our Lord and Savior. As for everyone else, heed the same advice. Don't worry about what you have no control over. It's just wasted time.

A pastor once told me some life-changing advice. He said, "C.J., I've seen God move because of faith, but I've never seen Him move because of emotions." Me, worrying and crying all day, doesn't make God move any faster on my behalf. Hebrews 11:6 reads, "But without faith it is impossible to please Him, for he who comes to God must believe that He is, and that He is a rewarder of those who diligently seek Him." So stop worrying; you would have been better served by allocating those thoughts toward something positive.

Satan doesn't want you to be free. He knows that making you worry keeps you stagnant. It paralyzes you before the next move. God told me to bless my spiritual brother with a semi-huge amount of money and I followed the order. For days on end, the devil kept speaking to me. He would say things like, "You know you just blew that money." "God didn't tell you to do anything. You're an idiot." See, the enemy knows that I am stronger in my walk. He can't just place simple temptations in my face to make me walk off the path. I'm not an easy target anymore. I fight back, or at least I try to fight back. Now he has upped the ante and sends attacks to my decisions. He can't make me move, so now he tries to confuse me. He just speaks lies to me, all day. Before I used to pray, and I would get this spiritual confirmation on things. In the midst of confusion, I would ask God for direction or confirmation. I would then get a feeling inside, a visual confirmation, or hear words spoken to me. Not this time. At my present moment, I have been praying against the mental attacks, and God hasn't responded the way He had before. I feel like Jesus being tempted in the wilderness. When it happened, God didn't send angels down to protect Jesus. Jesus already knew what was the right thing to do, He just had to stick to the truth.

When I was praying over the money I gave up, God just said, "You heard my voice the first time I told you to do it." Then He gave me Psalms 23:4. It reads, "Yea, though I walk through the valley of the shadow of death, I will fear no evil; For You are with me; Your rod and Your staff, they comfort me." Then the Holy Spirit quickly said, "You will walk through the valley of the shadow of death, but God is with you. Just trust, C.J." So this time around, I only have the truth to hold onto. I could worry that I made the wrong decision, but what good would that do? I know God told me to do it. Even if I made a mistake, can God not give me that money back? Is He not all-powerful? Can He not bless my heart? When did a green piece of paper, that society says has worth, get above the undeniable authority of Christ? It hasn't. So therefore, I don't worry about it; I just do my part. I praise God with my words and actions throughout the process, and look out for my blessings.

Our words are very important. We speak things into existence.

Proverbs 18:21 says, "Death and life are in the power of the tongue, and those who love it will eat its fruit." The words people say wield great power. For instance, most marriages that fail are from lack of communication or mutual respect. The God-given gift of marriage isn't tainted. We will treat strangers with the utmost respect, then come home and speak to our family like they are beneath us. I, too, have done this on many occasions. I apologize to my wife all the time for things I said when we first got married. Regardless if I was blaming her for something, voicing how I felt, or critiqued her work ethic within the marriage, I spoke death on her.

"What does that mean? " you ask? "They're just words." Let's look at the result. As I continued to speak down on my wife, those "words" took on a natural manifestation. Think about what I said earlier about your thoughts and actions. Those words became her thoughts. She first believed the lie that the devil had me speak to her. I didn't think she was a horrible person, but anybody being a fly on the wall would say otherwise. Out of my frustration, I would speak things that weren't true to the degree that I was saying them. I over exaggerated my emotions. She began to dwell upon the lies, accepting them as truth. Then that truth manifested its physical form in her life. She started to become insecure. She started to become depressed. She gained weight. That weight gain made her even more depressed. She felt trapped in a relationship with someone that wouldn't show love back to her. She started to give up on herself. I saw all of this with my own eyes. To be totally honest, I'm ashamed to say it but, I didn't even care. I was so selfish to where I would watch her suffer, and felt she deserved it. Like it was her punishment. That's so wrong.

God is faithful, though. He sent my parents to speak to me, not knowing what was going on in my relationship. That's how I know it was God. My parents spoke directly to my situation without knowing they were doing it. They told me to speak life to my wife. She isn't perfect, and neither am I. They told me to think about all the bad things that God could say about me and my actions. Even though He could say plenty, He doesn't. He just perfectly loves my imperfections. So I should keep the same spirit toward my wife. It hit home, and I haven't been the same since. Our relationship hasn't been the same since. Think about how far we had to come over "words" being spoken.

I remember my third grade teacher telling me that I wouldn't do anything with my life. She really meant what she said, and felt she was right for it. It hurt, but the reason it hit home was because her daughter was the smartest student in my grade. Her words spoke death to me. I almost gave up on trying, in the third grade, because of words spoken over me. The lie that was attached almost became my reality. The only thing that saved me were the words of my mother. I wasn't going to tell her, but I kept feeling this urge to do so. Now, I know it was the Holy Spirit. When I brought it up, she pulled me in really close and spoke, "You are a child of God, C.J. There isn't ANYTHING you can't do with the help of the Lord." She then forced me to tell myself that I could make grades just as high as that teacher's daughter. It was something about me speaking those words that changed the entire situation for myself. I began to believe what I was saying. Next thing I knew, she and I had similar grades at the end of the year. We would compete over homework assignment grades, and eventually I surpassed her. As I reflect back, I realize that that was a pivotal moment for me. Our words are important.

Most preachers speak about our words in the spiritual realm. They compare the power of our spoken words to when God spoke to create the world. I won't come at it from that angle. God wants me to speak about a certain situation that pertains to a woman at a church I previously attended. Her name is Sister Betty. She's an older lady, and she was diagnosed with a brain tumor. She had already beaten several complications in her life, including a stroke prior to the brain tumor diagnosis. This one shook her, though. The doctors told her she didn't have that long to live. She is a devout believer, and she lay across the altar every Sunday. She believed God could heal her, but that burden was extremely heavy to bear. One day after service, she and I began to talk about her situation. She never said she couldn't be healed, but her confidence was at an all-time low. As we talked, the Holy Spirit told me to speak and He would give me the words. I remember telling her that she was looking at this brain tumor thing all wrong. I told her to think about the testimony she would be able to give if God allowed her to make it through. Even with those doctors telling her that she was sure to die, I told her to walk in that office with her head high. She was a child of God, and He was placing her in a situation to reveal His glory.

I ended by telling her to not let fear make her speak death on herself. The thing is, how can God show his power without using someone in unbelievable circumstances? If she didn't have the brain tumor, she could tell people that God kept her healthy. Yet, those people could discredit God, saying that's normal. Walking amongst the same doctors and nurses, who said she wouldn't live, and walking out of that hospital alive is a miracle before their eyes. That's how faith is built. If we speak doubt during our time of faith, we will belittle our relationship with God. To a non-believer, it will seem that God didn't heal you because of your faith. How could it, when you didn't show any faith when you spoke to them? It's a bold move to look death in the face and peacefully say that God's will is sufficient. Sister Betty lit up on the inside and I knew she received God's words spoken through me. His words gave her peace to trust Him in the supernatural realm. Needless to say, the very next check-up, the doctors told her that the brain tumor was gone. When she told me, I started to cry with her. I get so moved when I see God do great wonders in the world.

It hurts my heart that so many people still don't believe in Jesus. His teachings are true, and His power is unlimited. That's why I take to my heart what He says in Matthew 12:36, "But I say to you that for every idle word men may speak, they will give account of it in the day of judgment." I'm still praying daily over my mouth. My words get reckless at times. God is changing me from my experiences, through revelation. The Holy Spirit broke down some key points to me when I was in conversation with the Lord. He said Jesus used His physical actions to heal people, but He spoke to the devil during his temptations. Some parents speak encouragement and blessings over their kids, while others speak derogatory comments throughout their lives. You speak to numerous people in a day, including your co-workers, girl-friend or boyfriend, random store clerk, guy walking down the street, etc. How many times have you walked up to one of these people and said, "Your outfit looks nice"? You gave them a compliment, not knowing what they did to deserve it. That person could have spent two hours in the mirror, and her spouse didn't even notice. The devil might have been attacking her insecurities, making her feel like crap. God then sends you to brighten her mood, because He loves her. He knew how much it was needed for that person to receive a compliment at that moment. He didn't physically change her mood. He allowed the natural law of "words" to speak life back into her. Those words spoken translate into actions. She can ride that compliment out for who knows how long. Her work day is more efficient, and her spirit shines on all that come in her path. All that from speaking a few kind words when you were prompted to do so.

Words do have a real effect on us, positive or negative. James 3:5-8 says,

> Even so the tongue is a little member and boasts great things. See how great a forest a little fire kindles! And the tongue is a fire, a world of iniquity. The tongue is so set among our members that it defiles the whole body, and sets on fire the course of nature; and it is set on fire by hell. For every kind of beast and bird, of reptile and creature of the sea, is tamed and has been tamed by mankind. But no man can tame the tongue. It is an unruly evil, full of deadly poison.

We can repress the impulses of animals through conditioning and reprimand, but the sinfulness that inspires evil words is beyond our control. Only the Holy Spirit within us can bring this fatal force under control. So capture your thoughts, and monitor your words. I sometimes read Colossians 4:6 when I make the mistake of speaking rudely to someone. It reads, "Let your speech always be with grace, seasoned with salt, that you may know how you ought to answer each one." So remember to speak positive words out of your mouth to yourself, and to one another.

God will deal with your strongholds before your behavior can change.

Satan doesn't want you to prosper at all. He wants you to curse people out, steal for what you need, live and die by your own decisions, etc. He wants you to live a life full of strongholds. God will break those strongholds down if you allow Him. Once those strongholds disappear, you will see growth. God is righteous; therefore, He has to make you aware of your evil actions. For example, before you can genuinely speak kindly to people, regardless of how they treat you, God has to change your heart. You might think that's not the case, but think back to the last time you were really upset. Did you want to talk to anyone at that time? No, why not? Because you were pissed off, that's why. When the enemy has us feeling some type of way, we shut down. A great man of God once asked me, "How can you be effective for the Kingdom of God, and easily get offended at people?" He was dead on. Me taking offense was a stronghold in my life. I was still spreading my faith with people, but I was hindered in what I could do. The moment somebody said something slick, I was flying off the handle. That didn't change my relationship with God, it just showed Him what I needed to work on.

Another thing I am working on now is when fellow believers come to me and tell me their opinions about my life. I'm a rough dude. In the streets, you can't just run up to somebody and tell them what you think about them. You might get shot. For some reason, people feel that because we both follow Jesus, they can say what they want to me. That's definitely not the case. What they can do is present to me what the Holy Spirit tells them to, in the right way.

Look at King David in the bible. In Acts 13:22, God says, "I have found David the son of Jesse, a man after My own heart, who will do all My will." God blessed him in everything that he did. David was a great king, and his army conquered many areas. Deep down though, he had strong-holds that God had to bring to the forefront. I'm going to give you the short version of his trials. David sees a woman named Bathsheba and invites her to his palace. He wants to have sex with her. She is married to a man named Uriah, who is off fighting the war for King David and his fellow people. She ends up getting pregnant. At this point, David could have just fessed up and told everyone what happened. We don't know why he didn't, but he chose to try and cover up his actions. He had Uriah leave the battlefield and come home for a few days. He figured Uriah would have sex with Bathsheba and think she was pregnant with his own child. Uriah refuses to sleep with his wife. He doesn't want to enjoy pleasure while his people are suffering through a war. Then David tries to get Uriah drunk, but it still doesn't work. So finally, David decides to have Uriah killed. David sends Uriah back to the war with a message for the commander. The message is for the commander to place Uriah on the front lines of the battle. He ends up getting killed. David then marries his wife, Bathsheba.

God was not pleased with David's actions. God knew that David was a good man; He said David was a man after His own heart. That's a huge testament to David's internal make-up. However, this certain stronghold needed to be addressed. The Lord sent the prophet Nathan to David. The way Nathan revealed what God needed to show David was extraordinary. We all can learn from his approach. Nathan presented to David a parable. He says in 2 Samuel 12:1-4,

> There were two men in one city, one rich and
> the other poor. The rich man had exceedingly
> many flocks and herds. But the poor man had
> nothing, except one little ewe lamb which
> he had bought and nourished; and it grew up
> together with him and with his children. It

ate of his own food and drank from his own cup and lay in his bosom; and it was like a daughter to him. And a traveler came to the rich man, who refused to take from his own flock and from his own herd to prepare one for the wayfaring man who had come to him; but he took the poor man's lamb and prepared it for the man who had come to him.

David became extremely angry. He told Nathan, "As the Lord lives, the man who has done this shall surely die! And he shall restore fourfold for the lamb, because he did this thing and because he has no pity." Then Nathan told David, "You are the man!"

Nathan came at David out of love, which allowed God to work on David's heart. The Lord had to deal with David's strongholds before they could move forward. Consequences were attached to David's sin, but God didn't cut David off from His love and mercy. This passage of scriptures helps me with my stronghold of pride. We tend to pass judgment and criticize each other when we feel the need to comment on each other's lives. Pride produces resentment, which places another stronghold on the individual. I am still learning how to not get offended when people overstep their boundaries with me. Like I said earlier, strongholds have to be dealt with before our behavior can change. I thank God that He has brought me a mighty long way.

Before we go to the next section, let me clear the air. I'm all for the Christian community keeping each other in line. The bible says in Mark 12:30-31 that, "You shall love the Lord your God with all your heart, with all your soul, with all your mind, and with all your strength. This is the first commandment. And the second, like it, is this: 'You shall love your neighbor as yourself.' There is no other commandment greater than these." If you wanted to sum up everything that Jesus requires us to do, while living on earth, you could in those two scriptures. With loving your neighbor comes the assignment of helping him or her stay focused on the requirements of God. I get it. I am my brother's keeper. At the same time, I don't agree with believers condemning other believers, as if they are above them because of their "spiritual deeds." If you beat a stronghold, God bless you. If you want to help another person be released from the same stronghold, more power to you. If you are destroying another human being's spirit by quoting every biblical scripture your little brain has memorized, in order to condemn another person's walk, you can kick rocks. I hate to be cliché, but only God can judge me.

Romans 14:1-13 says,

> Receive one who is weak in the faith, but not to disputes over doubtful things. For one believes he may eat all things, but he who is weak eats only vegetables. Let not him who eats despise him who does not eat, and let him who does not eat judge him who eats; for God has received him. Who are you to judge another's servant? To his own master he stands or falls. Indeed, he will be made to stand, for God is able to make him stand. One person esteems one day above another; another esteems every day alike. Let each be fully convinced in his own mind. He who observes the day, observes it to the Lord; and he who does not observe the day, to the Lord does he not observe it. He who eats, eats to the Lord, for he gives God thanks; and he who does not eat, to the Lord he does not eat, and gives God thanks. For none of us lives to himself, and no one dies to himself. For

if we live, we live to the Lord; and if we die, we die to the Lord. Therefore, whether we live or die, we are the Lord's. For to this end Christ died and rose and lived again, that He might be Lord of both the dead and the living. But why do you judge your brother? Or why do you show contempt for your brother? For we shall all stand before the judgment seat of Christ. For it is written: "As I live, says the Lord, Every knee shall bow to Me, And every tongue shall confess to God." So then each of us shall give account of himself to God. Therefore let us not judge one another anymore, but rather resolve this, not to put a stumbling block or a cause to fall in our brother's way.

That's my thoughts exactly. God is working on all of us in His time, not my own. I'm not saying I can't be corrected; I'm just saying don't come at me like you're God in the flesh. We are all dirty, so let's just gently cleanse one another with the sponge of righteousness. Many times, God's people mean well when they quote the way we are supposed to live. Just make sure when someone is telling you their thoughts, that those thoughts line up with the Word of God.

If you don't resist people's wrong thoughts, you often will take them as your own thoughts.

The misconception I see when speaking to other believers is that most don't believe that the devil ever uses them. I'm not talking about demon possession, but more along the lines of "prompting to action." We sometimes speak out of our mouths things that are contrary to the Word of God. That's why you have to learn the voice of God for yourself.

Even when you go to church, and the pastor gives a remarkable sermon, you still should go to the bible to make sure his sermon was correct. You don't want to take someone's thoughts as your own unless you know them to be true.

For example, my wife and I regularly attended a church in Maryland. One Sunday, the pastor got up on the pulpit and said, "There are people here that say the Lord talks to them all the time. The Lord doesn't talk to any of us all the time. You know that was a lie from the devil." As soon as I heard that, I knew he was speaking from his own thoughts. How did I know? By lining up his words with what the bible says.

Believers and non-believers alike already know that God consists of the Holy Trinity. The Father, Son, and Holy Spirit are independent, yet still the same. So that would make sense when reading 2 Corinthians 3:17. It reads, "Now the Lord is the Spirit; and where the Spirit of the Lord is, there is liberty." The Holy Spirit is God Himself, like the Father and the Son. So why would we receive a Helper that never speaks to us? Jesus said in John 14:26, "But the Helper, the Holy Spirit, whom the Father will send in My name, He will teach you all things, and bring to your remembrance all things that I said to you." How does he teach us? John 16:13-14 reads, "However, when He, the Spirit of truth, has come, He will guide you into all truth; for He will not speak on His own authority, but whatever He hears He will speak; and He will tell you things to come." So in conclusion, part of the Holy Spirit's job is to SPEAK to us what the Father tells Him.

I'm not writing this to degrade the pastor, but the truth is the truth. I still wonder how many people heard that comment and believed it? He probably set back some of his own members who were actively seeking the face of God. That's why it's important to be aware of Satan's attacks at all times. He will use anybody, or any given situation, if allowed. People always speak their thoughts about you, even when you don't ask them. We have to make sure we capture whatever thoughts arise in our own brain from their thought expression. If not, the enemy will have you living a defeated life.

After college, I wanted to move to New York and attend an acting school. I told my family my plans, and they bombarded me with reasons why I shouldn't go. They told me every statistic from acting failures to fatality rates. At first I wanted to believe them. They're my parents, so I figured they knew more than I did. Then as I started to inquire as to where there concerns derived from, I realized it was from fear. Neither of them had been to New York. The only time they had seen the big city of bright lights was when they watched *CSI: NY* on television. They did have genuine concerns about my safety, but in the end, they were projecting their fears upon me. I had to realize that God had His own plan for my life. I knew I had to go. That experience changed my life. I can only imagine how my life would have played out if I stayed back in Alabama instead of moving to New York. Many of you reading this have been praying for changes in your life. You can't be afraid to take the necessary steps toward those changes. You may not get the response of support that you wanted from the people around you, but that's okay.

In Genesis 12:1-2, the Lord told Abram (Abraham before the name change), "Get out of your country, from your family and from your father's house, to a land that I will show you. I will make you a great nation; I will bless you and make your name great; and you shall be a blessing." Abram was content in the region where he resided. His family was his support, and in his father's house he had leadership responsibility. God commanded Abram to leave all these things in which he found comfort. He was asked to go to a place that God wouldn't even define until Abram got there. God didn't tell everyone to move, He just told Abram. What if Abram held a village meeting and asked the group their opinion? He would have been given all types of reasons to stay in his present location. Satan would have worked that entire meeting because he hates to see God walk His children into their blessings. The devil would have made sure the thoughts and fears of the group were projected onto Abram. Their negativity could have deterred Abram from listening to God and His directions.

I'm not telling you to act upon every thought you get, but to balance that thought against the Word of God. Make sure that voice you hear belongs to the Lord. You have to be mindful of who you are listening to, and what you take in. Also, negative thoughts will come back if you don't fill up the empty space with positive thinking. When I begin my workout on the treadmill, I'm in my zone. My body feels good, and my mind feels strong. As my heart rate starts to increase, I keep myself motivated by listening to music. It keeps my mind off of the pain that is slowly creeping into my muscles and joints. Then the breaking point occurs. My run pace slows down and I start to breathe heavily. This is the moment that will make or break my workout. I speak motivational encouragement to myself as I push through. I get so amped on my own words and thoughts. I try to ride that wave of momentum to the end of the workout. Now I'm running in silence, feeling good that I made it over the hurdle. Two minutes ago, I almost quit. Next thing you know, I hear this voice in my head say, "C.J., you are about to fall out. This workout is too intense. Just stop and pick it up another day." Now I have a choice. I can denounce the thought and continue to push through the suck, or listen to it and quit. Sometimes I win, sometimes I lose. On the days I would stop, I felt like crap afterward. Here I am asking God to help me get motivated to lose weight; then when I'm doing the workout, I quit. The devil sits back and laughs. He knows how much my weight loss means to me. He knows that I could have finished. He just spoke a word and I believed it. That's why it's important that you continue to speak positivity into your spirit. Words have power. My mistake was thinking that I could speak a couple seconds of motivational words to myself, and those words would hold me for the remainder of my workout. When

I quit motivating myself, the devil slipped in and replaced my positivity with his negativity.

You can't decide to be the best teacher in the world without encouraging yourself through the obstacles. If you think encouragement is not needed, just look to your left and right. How many people do you see with dreams and aspirations, yet they are stagnant? They constantly get defeated and ask God for assistance. He tells them what road to travel, but that road is a very long road. They don't want to stay focused and work hard. They want rewards without effort. The biblical book of James says, "Faith without works is dead." So faith is necessary to get through the trying times in your life. Romans 10:17 says, "So then faith comes by hearing, and hearing by the word of God." Faith comes by hearing the Word of God, and speaking it boldly to yourself. Those are our promises.

In my early teens, my father and I traveled extensively. He was an umpire and called games all over, including the Little League World Series. In between his games, sometimes he would have to attend meetings with other umpires. He trusted me to behave, so he would tell me to stay in a certain location. As I waited, people would ask me if I was lost. They didn't understand why I was sitting so contently in one area. I would tell them I was waiting on my father. Due to his work ethic, everybody in the park knew him. They would tell me that my father was around the corner. I knew they meant well, but I never budged. My father told me to stay, and I received that. I didn't waiver in my thoughts because someone else told me something different. No matter how close their advice was to what my father told me to do, I didn't let it make me disregard my father's command. When I would begin to waiver, thinking I should get up, I just spoke back what my father told me to do. That's how we are to be with God's word. When times get hard and confusing, you may want to jump ship. You'll start listening to anybody, hoping they will have the magic key to help you get through. God already gave that to us. The bible is full of things God promises us, including the guarantee that a believer is "dead indeed to sin, but alive to God in Christ Jesus."

The old you died to Christ, and now you are new.

Let's go back to the last statement about monitoring who you should decide to speak to during a crisis. There are many of you who have received Jesus into your hearts, but you are still bound because of your current relationships. Before you accepted Jesus, you might have made decisions based upon the opinions of the people that surrounded you. Now that you seek God's guidance, the things He might show you may not line up with the advice your friends used to give you in the past. I'm not saying the advice given to you by your friends is bad because they might not be saved. I've been around numerous Christians that have given the worst advice in history! Even though the Word of God gives us a foundation, it doesn't replace common sense. In all honesty, it adds to it.

The old you, the "slave to sin" you, is spiritually dead and buried. The thing is, we keep digging our old nature back up. There are people reading this that think they are still dead, but they can walk out of their grave at any time. For many, you can't get out of the grave because everybody around you is having a party in that same grave. I will use one of my friends as an example. He and his wife received Jesus into their lives about two years ago. They have a young son. Their son was conceived before their acceptance of the Lord. During that time, they raised him without any type of reprimand. He was an awful child. He would tear things up, yell at them, throw things, and make their lives a living hell. They didn't know what to do, so they sought out answers from their close friends and family. Since they questioned such a large group, the responses varied. Many of the parents that were questioned also had bad children. They decided to listen to a close friend, because they trusted her. She told them it was a phase, and that the son would grow out of it. They believed her advice, and operated under her words. The little boy grew worse. He was a tyrant. After a while, they got fed up with the son's lack of discipline. Instead of going back to that same source of bad information, they decided to pray over the ordeal. God placed it on their hearts to call me.

After hearing their situation, I prayed and spoke what God gave me. Before we break this principle down, I just want to reiterate that all of God's promises and commands have a purpose. He will not tell us to do something, or stay away from something, unless it is of the utmost importance. With that being said, I told my friend he needed to quit being lazy and discipline his child. He replied that he and his wife didn't believe in punishing their children. After he finished, I asked him one important question: "How is that working out for you?" He wanted to say a response, but he couldn't. He knew I was right. I told him I wanted to not only show him the scripture that states it, but also scriptures that support the principle. Proverbs 13:24 says, "He who spares his rod hates his son, but he who loves him disciplines him promptly." Kids are always going to try their parents in some way. They are learning what boundaries are around them. We all do it throughout our lives. I told him that the reason God requires us to provide that discipline for our kids is in Proverbs 29:15. It reads, "The rod and rebuke give wisdom, but a child left to himself brings shame to his mother." The purpose for punishing your son's bad behavior is to give him wisdom by knowing what is good behavior. It gives him an understanding that what he is doing is the wrong thing. That's part of your job, as a parent, so that your kid(s) can operate properly in society.

He then asked me, what good would come out of beating his child? I replied, "I never said beat your children." Many people think chastising your child means to go back to slavery days. Nobody deserves to be severely beaten, ever. Colossians 3:21 clearly states, "Fathers, do not provoke your children, lest they become discouraged." You can't overdue the punishment, because it will void out the purpose. You punish a child to teach a life lesson, not to get out your raging emotions. Then I said, "Look at it this way. Would you rather deal with these issues now, or deal with them for the remainder of your life?" Proverbs 29:17 reads, "Correct your son, and he will give you rest; Yes, he will give delight to your soul." I asked him to think about when he and his wife go out on date nights. How many people do you see with unruly teenagers? How many times have you looked at someone else's child and wanted to discipline them yourself? He said, "Plenty." I replied, "That's what the scripture means. God tells us to deal with it now, or deal with the consequences later...our choice."

He listened to me intently, and I could tell his mind was going a mile a minute. I closed out our conversation with Proverbs 22:6, which reads, "Train up a child in the way he should go, and when he is old he will not depart from it." This is part of the responsibility when raising children. They can't train themselves. My friend told me, Thank you for the Godly advice." Right after we hung up, I told God, "Thank you for answering my prayer, by giving me the words to say." The Holy Spirit replied, "Do you know the main reason why God requires you to discipline your children?" I spoke back, "No." Then the Holy Spirit told me to look over at my bible. It was opened to the book of Hebrews. As I started to search for what He was showing me, I came across Hebrews 12:7-8: "If you endure chastening, God deals with you as with sons; for what son is there whom a father does not chasten? But if you are without chastening, of which all have become partakers, then you are illegitimate and not sons." As I read, the Holy Spirit said, "What you are doing is preparing your children for what their heavenly Father will do for them in their lifetime. You see, children are disciplined by their parents out of love. When done properly, they should learn from the discipline. God disciplines us with the same thing in mind." That blew me away. I immediately emailed that to my friend.

Later that night, I sat down and contemplated my friend's situation. I was thankful that he called me, but I also wondered, what if he hadn't called? What if he denied the urge to call me, and instead went to "old faithful"? That same friend might have given him some more bogus advice. To us, it's just advice. To Satan, it's a way to keep you bound and in the grave. My friend and his wife started to discipline their son, and now he has grown into a very well-mannered young man. He has come a long way. That might not have been the case if they continued to lie in their graves.

God has numerous ways to change your situations. The thing is, though, you can't be lazy. Accepting Christ doesn't instantly change you. It gives you a spiritual parent and His guidelines on how to live a prosperous and righteous life. How can you live if you are still taking advice from people that are dead? How can you live if you continue to do your old actions? Same actions produce the same results. This applies to everyone. I don't have to know if Warren Buffet is saved to learn from him how to manage my stock portfolio. He has a proven track record in the area. All I need to know is if what he did to gain his wealth, aligns with the Word of God. If so, I'll take the direction. If you are struggling with a sexual sin, don't go around your friends that always want to go get laid. If you don't want to do drugs anymore, quit going to pick up drugs with your friends, even if you don't use them. Why willingly walk into Satan's traps? Maybe one day, you will be strong enough to kick it with those people. Maybe one day, you'll look up and be around a new group of people. Either way, we have to strive to do better.

We are old in our sinful ways, but new in our love for Jesus. I promise you, this journey is tough. I always go back and forth, between the old and new me. I can truly say that I can see a difference. My belief is different, and my relationship with God gets stronger daily. I have transitioned into trying to make decisions based upon God's direction, instead of my own. It is a process, but the first step is knowing that I am a new creature. I live to be more like Jesus; that's it. If I can kill off one sinful desire a day, ranging from over-eating to thinking sexual thoughts, then I can consider that day a success.

We have to give God praise now.

Referring back to the scripture I quoted earlier from the book of Psalms that says, "Yea, though I walk through the valley of the shadow of death, I will fear no evil; For You are with me," valleys of death can translate to any obstacles in our lives. We know our existence comes with death, destruction and turmoil. These things are balanced by gifts from God, including love, trust, intimacy, etc. God knows the devil is going to come at you. He prepared us with warnings, followed by directions on how to cope, and ending with a promise that we could put our faith in Him.

For example, the bible reveals the plans of the devil in 1 Peter 5:8-9. "Be sober, be vigilant; because your adversary the devil walks about like a roaring lion, seeking whom he may devour. Resist him, steadfast in the faith, knowing that the same sufferings are experienced by your brotherhood in the world." Right there, we know it's coming. The bible tells us to resist him. Then the Word of God tells us in John 10:10, "The thief does not come except to steal, and to kill, and to destroy. I have come that they may have life, and that they may have it more abundantly." Jesus clearly tells us why he gave us this insider's knowledge on the devil. He tells you His purpose, compared to Satan's agenda. In John 3:16, it says, "For God so loved the world that He gave His only begotten Son, that whoever believes in Him should not perish but have everlasting life." He is telling us to hold on. There is more than meets the eye, when it comes to the variables that surround human existence. That's confirmation that He will give us the ultimate gift in the end.

So what does that mean to the believer? It means that God has your best interests at heart. What God do you know that sends His Son to the slaughter, to atone for the sins of His creations? If He did that, then why would He leave you in your most critical hour? The Word of God is truth. The problem is, we lose our faith during the storm. We get off the float, because we feel our parade of life is too long. Then God comes through, like He always does, and we try to get back on the float. We want to stand tall and accept the praise of others, as if we had had unwavering faith the entire time. I'm guilty of this myself. God wants us to praise Him before, during, and after...EVERYTHING! He wants you to fully trust that He is real in the natural, and working in the supernatural. The devil is totally opposite. He wants you to focus on the natural, hoping you won't notice him working in the supernatural to devour you. He wants to overwhelm and confuse you. Don't believe the lies.

Praise God because He is deserving of it. Don't do it just because you want your prayers to be answered. That's only part of it. Don't only praise Him after you get your college degree, or when your child is born. He loved you even when everybody in your college class thought you were an idiot. They might have passed judgment on you, but God didn't. He helped you be who you were all along. He created you. When your parents said you would never be able to raise a child, He showed you how to do it. He prepared you, so that you could prepare your seed. Again, He is faithful. We have to praise Him, even when we can't see the outcome. He has given us more than enough testimonies about His power. What more do you need? From historical records, all the way up to modern times, people have seen God's power work in their lives. He is the living God. If you have ever seen God move in a miraculous way in your life, you know what I mean about God's power. Why would you ever doubt it? Because we believe the enemy's lies, that's why.

I was praying to God one day, complaining about my financial status. This was like the fifth time I had prayed for this particular thing. God spoke to me, saying, "I heard you the first time. How many times are you going to pray about the same thing? Just have faith, and go forth." He was right. Did I think that God was deaf? Did I feel like I didn't pray loud enough the first time? Either way, He clearly told me what to do. So my only direction was to go forth, and that's what I have been doing ever since. When times got hard, He told me to trust and worship Him, regardless of what my physical eyes could see. The reason He said that was because I wasn't ready to receive my big, financial blessing. My heart and motives weren't lined up with God's, when it came to money. He had to teach me how to use it as a tool, before He would trust me with it. This trek has been long and rough. If I didn't trust God's direction, I would have quit a long time ago. I would have reverted to my own way of providing for my family.

As my wife and I have embarked on this road of faith, God has given us more than we could have asked for. He had people and companies bless us financially, without us even having to lift a finger. I'm so serious. Nobody can tell me the power of God isn't real. I see it work with my own eyes and it still amazes me when it happens. From these instances, my faith is built. This allows me to have a reference point when times get rough. That reference point pushes me to praise Him through the storm. He has provided for me time and time again. Why would this time be any different? I just seek His guidance, and wait on the answer. As I wait, I praise God. When the enemy sends people to discourage me, I look them right in the eyes and say, "God got me! I'm good!" That's it. They might call me crazy, stupid, I don't care. I praise God, no matter how bleak it looks. He is capable of any and all things.

We have to remain positive. We have to keep positive expectations, and engage in positive conversation. Take the short story of Hannah in the beginning of the book 1 Samuel. This was a woman who knew how to praise God through her most trying circumstances. Her praise wasn't always pretty, but genuine nonetheless. She couldn't get pregnant because God had closed her womb. She didn't know the reason why she was infertile. We only know the dialogue that was recorded in the scriptures. We don't know what words she sent up to God during this time. She could have yelled and cursed God, like many do today. Due to being a woman, she could have felt entitled, since pregnancy is a natural thing for women. She could have asked God, "What's wrong with me?" Again, we will never know. What we do see within the scriptures are the fruits of her spirit. She saw God as all-powerful. She still submitted her issue to His authority. In verse eleven, Hannah makes a vow to God, saying, "O Lord of hosts, if You will indeed look on the affliction of Your maidservant and remember me, and not forget Your maidservant, but will give your maidservant a male child, then I will give him to the Lord all the days of his life, and no razor shall come upon his head."

We don't know why God was holding her pregnancy back. Maybe she needed to give her son up to God in her heart. How many women reading this have had difficulty getting pregnant? You might have told God the same thing that Hannah did, but did you mean it? If God granted you that baby, then twenty years later, God allowed cancer to take him or her away for souls to come to Christ, would you still be happy with God? If no, does that mean you really would give up your son to Christ and His will? That could have been her issue. I don't know. Hannah didn't try to figure it out, though. She just kept the faith. We know this because she endured ridicule from the other women for not being pregnant, yet she still believed that God could change it.

In verse seven, it says that Hannah went up to Shiloh, year after year, with her husband. Shiloh was the religious center for the nation at that time. They went up there to worship and sacrifice to God. She remained faithful, every year. She could have stopped praising God a long time before. When confronted with deep pain, most people do quit on God. However, Hannah was loyal. She continued to worship God, even though the other women made her feel miserable because of her inability to procreate. She praised God through it. That praise wasn't singing songs and clapping hands. She was hurting, and yearning for a male child to give to her husband. Verse ten says, "And she was in bitterness of soul, and prayed to the Lord and wept in anguish." She didn't hide her pain, or act like she wasn't hurt. God is with us always. He knew how she felt. He knows how you feel. Psalms 62:8 says, "Trust in Him at all times, you people; Pour out your heart before Him; God is a refuge for us." He understands our suffering and our deepest desires. Hannah wasn't negotiating with God. By Hannah requesting a child from God, she was expressing her faith. She knew only God could open her womb. By saying she would give her child back to God, she was acknowledging that God would first provide a child. By praising God through her obstacles, she got to see God at His best. She stayed positive. She might have been a wreck, but she still kept her focus on God. She believed in positive expectations, and engaged in positive conversation with the Lord. Her result: a beautiful baby boy named Samuel.

Hannah also kept her promise to God after her pregnancy. After weaning him, she took Samuel with her to Shiloh. In front of the other worshippers, Hannah offered up her sacrifices to God. She then yelled out, "For this child I prayed, and the Lord has granted me my petition which I asked of Him. Therefore I also have lent him to the Lord; as long as he lives he shall be lent to the Lord." Hannah gave her testimony about what God had done for her. She exalted Him for his grace during her trial. She never lost her faith, praising Him from the request to the manifestation. Don't give up on God. He's always on time.

Continually saying "What if" brings on fear and negative thinking.

Do you know that God doesn't make mistakes? Romans 8:28 says, "All things work together for good to those who love God, to those who are the called according to His purpose." God has a purpose for your life, and that purpose aligns with His ultimate purpose for humanity. You have free will, so you make your own decisions. God knows what you will decide, but He can't make the decision for you. I want to give you a visual representation.

When I was growing up, I was really good at sports, particularly football. I always made the all-star teams, and produced at an elite level. My freshman year in high school, I became the captain on my football team. I played linebacker, and had a monster year. I was the team's second leading tackler, and we ended up losing in the championship game. I did so well that the coaches wanted me to try out for varsity instead of junior varsity. I still had a small body frame compared to the juniors and seniors on the varsity team, but that didn't deter me. I went out on that practice field, convinced that I would get me a spot. When my name was called during seven-on-seven drills, I stepped up. The center hiked the ball, and the quarterback handed it off to the running back. He hit the hole hard, but I met him there. BAM! I put my all into the hit, and it stung him for a quick second. My body was too small, though, and he continued to go forward. I held on for dear life, and he fell on top of me. I was ecstatic. My first time practicing with varsity, and I hit their top running back in the hole. I expected my coaches to be thrilled with my performance. I let the running back get up, but before I could follow, the varsity defensive coach ran up to me. He yelled in my face, "You call that a f**king hit? You let him run you over. Get off my f**king field." Just like that, my confidence was shot. Those words cut so deeply that I quit playing football altogether.

Let me make it known—that was my decision. God didn't tell me to quit. I chose to. That was my first mistake. Before everyone knew I had quit, my name was circulating around the school. They had heard about me ballin' my freshman year, and my popularity sky-rocketed. The devil sent several women in my direction, and that stamped me quitting. I wanted to focus on my sexual desires instead of developing my God-given gift. That was my second mistake. I arrogantly decided that I was good enough to take my sophomore year off, and pick football back up my junior year. Little did I know that I would tear my rotator cuff my junior year, right before the football season started. Now I was upset. I yelled at God, saying it was His fault. I felt that because He is God, He should have kept me from the injury. It definitely wasn't His fault. Looking back, He sent several people to get me back on track when I first thought about quitting. I didn't heed their advice. So my senior year I went out to play football again, but I was forced to quit by my parents. The surgery I had done on my rotator cuff was very intricate. The doctor told my parents that if were to get hit in the sweet spot, my shoulder could give out and undo what was surgically done. Needless to say, I was devastated. Just like that, my dream was gone.

On top of that, I graduated high school and went to college at the University of Alabama. We've always had a decent football team, but my freshman year, they were on probation. The NCAA limited the amount of scholarships that the University of Alabama could give out to potential student-athletes. I could have joined the team as a walk-on. I was finally on my own. My parents couldn't tell me not to do it. Everything in me said to go try out. I couldn't accept God's voice. I felt that if these guys played football on national television, it was for a reason. Based on that principle alone, I sold myself short.

This is the kicker. My school has placed numerous players in the NFL, many of whom I know from my time attending the university. For example, Roman Harper, the safety who played for the New Orleans Saints and Carolina Panthers, was in my freshman class. He was good, but he hadn't grown into his full abilities. No disrespect to him, but he wasn't better than me. So watching him go through the ranks, from a benchwarmer to a starter, I was sick. Again, I was furious with God, as if He was the reason I couldn't play football. When Roman Harper got drafted, I was done. I was past my window of opportunity, while I watched people I knew make a living off of their gifts. Those thoughts continued to spiral more and more out of control. Each year, when the NFL draft would come on, I would get so depressed. Football was my love, but I didn't treat it as such when I had the opportunity. I kept contemplating the "what ifs." Fast forward to 2014, and I have a new perspective. I know that my athleticism was from God. The love for football was all mine. I was thankful that He gave me the ability to play the sport.

For many years, I questioned if my actions changed my cards. To be honest, they did. The way you perceive that answer may differ from the way I do. Again, we make our own decisions. I could have stayed faithful with football, and played my way to the NFL. I could have played in college, and hurt my shoulder worse than what it was already. I don't know. Either way, God is faithful. He is still in control. That means, even if I did quit football, He still blessed me through my other abilities. You can dig yourself in a hole, and it's nothing for God to put His hand down to pull you up. God's help can consist of someone He sends in the natural, internal motivation to climb out, or a divine miracle. He's capable of anything. You dug the hole, not God. That's your free will. He helped you out. That's divine power. After you get out of the hole, you have a choice. You can say, "I don't want to endure anymore random holes in my life. Hey God, can you help me with my life?" He will guide you. On the contrary, you could say, "I'm free, so what do I do now? You know what, I'm going to dig another hole. That's what I'm good at doing." Then you get stuck in the consequences of your own decisions. Next thing you know, it's *Groundhog Day* again.

You begin to live in a cycle that never takes you anywhere. That's what happened with football. I started making my own decisions. I dug my own hole. When He took me out, I made another hole. One hole was called arrogance and the other hole was called fear. Both aren't from God. Back then, I didn't know the Word of God like I do now. I killed my future, because I was stuck in the past. I was stuck in the "'what if' zone." Understand, you have to make decisions. We know that. God knew that I would blow my chance at football. That didn't stop Him from allowing me the time I did have with the sport. I should have been thankful. Think about it. God could have said, "C.J., that was your only chance to be successful. Now you have to live on this earth in poverty. That was your only gift." He said nothing of the sort. He still blessed me. He still allowed me to grow in other gifts that were given to me. Going back to the scripture written earlier, God made "all things work together for the good to those who love God." He allowed me to join the military and deploy to a foreign country. I met my wife. She alone was worth me joining the Army.

Maybe one day, I'll be able to see my kids do something spectacular in their lives. That would be amazing. I would take that over any accolades I could ever receive on my own abilities. God knows that, though. He knows, because of what I went through, that I will prepare my kids to stay focused. He knows that I will have them place God first in their lives.

If they know His plans are for them to prosper, then they will trust in His will. They won't get stagnant because of the "what ifs." They will trust that nothing is by accident. God is always in control. If He can make the universe, I'm sure He can bring you into whatever season He promised you. You just have to humbly ask for direction and listen. That's it. Can you believe it's that easy? Many of you reading don't believe that, and never will. It really is that easy, though. God didn't make salvation hard for us to attain. All He asked was that we receive Jesus into our hearts, and have faith in His promise of eternal life. He would take care of the rest. The same goes with the "what ifs." God just wants you to trust that nothing that happens to you is coincidental. I know this might be beyond our scope of understanding, but God created the universe. We can't grasp the power He possesses, and the infinite realm that He operates in. In this regard, our minds are like those of children.

If you walk up to your five-year-old son and tell him: "Son, you need to get prepared. One day in the future, you will have a wife and kids. You will be married, and have to stay loyal to your spouse. The devil will try to guide you to commit adultery, or mistreat your kids. You need to be prepared for this, son." He's gonna look back at you with a face full of bewilderment. He has no clue what you are talking about. His brain can't grasp marriage. He doesn't comprehend adultery, but these things are still true. One day, they will come to pass in his life. That's how we have to view the Word of God. We can't ask God to show us everything, right now. He will show you in due time. You can't live in the past, thinking about that one fork in the road, where you decided to go left instead of right. "What ifs" don't change reality. The devil will have you destroy your life before it ever starts. There are numerous people in the world that wake up and go to sleep, still living in their high school success. That used to be me. You think you are living life, but your life revolves around the old you.

You're so stuck in the "'what if' zone" that you totally neglect the "'This Is NOW' zone!" You are so mad at God because you feel that you missed out on something. You can't even see your blessing right down the road.

I spent so many years feeling down about my football career that I couldn't see God pushing me toward my creative side. I was eventually able to run my own multimedia company, Lucid Bleu Entertainment. I have shot commercials and music videos. I manage music artists. I wrote this book. I have been able to hone my other talents. God gave me those too. The thing is, this time I won't let my opportunities slip away. I don't ask "what if" when thinking about failure. I just go forth. I let the cards fall where they may. I am really working to get to a spot where I don't question anything from the Lord. I want to trust Him wholeheartedly. That's the only way I can be an effective leader. Nobody wants to come to a football huddle and hear the quarterback speaking doubt. They want the leader to speak victory. They can't win if they focus on the "what ifs." They have to play hard, and leave it all on the field. That's where we should place our focus.

Many will say that slumps occur for different reasons.

What does that mean? Instead of defining the statement, I want to make you think. Ask yourself, what's God's plan for humanity? We know there are layers to that answer. Think about when a couple decides to have kids. If asked why they had kids, they might give numerous reasons. The wife might want to experience childbirth, the father secretly might want to live out his dreams through his son or daughter, and/or they both just might want to live out society's status quo: married, kids, and a big house with a dog and a picket fence. Compare that to your vision of God. Many of us wake up every day watching the lives of everyone around us. We then come to God, asking for what we see. We turn on the television and see Oprah and her wealth, and then we pray to God for wealth. Then we go on throughout our day, waiting on God to instantly give us wealth. As the days continue, we grow weary with waiting. Finally, we either decide to ambitiously get it ourselves, or we accept our impoverished state. Neither decision is from God.

That's not the reason God created us; that's only a part. He created us to worship Him. He created us to be in an intimate relationship with Him for the entirety of our existence. I know we all have slumps in our lives. We are constantly in a boxing match with the enemy, and sometimes those rounds go on forever. It's not always a clean fight. We do get beat up from time to time. When you look at it, though, what we call "slumps" aren't really slumps. One Corinthians 13:11 says, "When I was a child, I spoke as a child, I understood as a child, I thought as a child; but when I became a man, I put away childish things." Even in my adult state, if all I do is ask God for "things" and complain when I don't receive them; I'm no better than a spoiled seven-year-old child.

Many view not instantly getting what they request from God as a slump. Is it really, though? God did promise to prosper us, but what does that really mean to you? When you promise to provide for your children, what does that mean? It means you will cover their needs, and their wants. Does a good parent give their children everything they ask for? Not right off the bat. If your child asks for his first car at the age of ten, do you immediately run out to purchase it? No, even if you could. What you would do is tell him there's an order in place. He has to learn how to drive. If the car he wanted was past your budget, you wouldn't be able to buy it. Does that mean he will never have the car? Absolutely not. You two could come up with a plan to make the purchase happen. You might cover a portion of the cost, but tell him to work and cover the other half. Even if you had the money, you still might make him work for it. You might want him to understand what it takes to attain such things, so that he appreciates your gratitude. Ultimately, what does all that mean? You are teaching him life lessons. You are being intimate with your creations, your kids. So why is it that we think we are above children as adults, yet we still act as such?

What you call "slumps," God calls parenting. He is parenting His children. His lessons are on a spiritual level. That's where He transcends us in a supernatural space. So if hard work is required, then how can we call that a slump? How can we lose weight without working out? That's God's natural process for our bodies. However, we choose to take every diet pill on planet Earth to achieve results. I'm all for the use of certain medicines to help the process, but you still have to go to the gym and endure the suck. The pain and time dedicated to your goals not only helps you achieve them, but it builds you for the next challenge. He is building us on numerous levels, but we only see what's right in front of us. We're the child that cries because our father said we couldn't get the car right now. We pout and express our attitude to everyone around us. Even if you don't curse God, not trusting is just as sinful. We are denying God the privilege of grooming us for life. He is our proud and loving Father. He deserves that right; He created us.

What we think is a slump, is usually a void that needs to be filled and satisfied with Jesus. While you are requesting prestige amongst your fellow men and women, He could be teaching you patience with your fellow men and women. That slump is really your season of preparation. When we are children, all we ever want is to grow up. We loathe the fact that our parents tell us what to do. We want to make our own decisions. When we get older, we begin to compare ourselves to others. When our comparison shows our lack in certain areas, we deny the vision by reverting to our childish ways. We say to ourselves, "I'm grown, and I'm me. I'm not changing for anybody." We think that when we start adulthood, the life lessons stop. Deep down we know that isn't the case, but we don't show it. We refuse to allow God to mold us. We fight with this constant desire to think that we know everything, and that we are in control. When you ask people that are older in age and close to death what they would change in their lives, their responses are almost unanimous. They all wish they would have loved more. They would have focused on the things that were of importance. Those things they speak of are the same things that God has been trying to reveal to us since the Garden of Eden. That apple Eve ate has us searching for this sense of control that forever eludes us. It's all false.

We think wealth will change us inwardly. We think being rude to one another justifies our feelings. We think God doesn't really have control. So now you have to decide if you really trust God, or do you just say you do? This war is real. This life is real. People are dying physical and spiritual deaths daily. They have believed the lies that the devil has placed before them. Instead of realizing that we are all children in Spirit when it comes to the Father, we take on the stature of Satan. We denounce the love and protection, because we want the control. We don't want to learn how to love. We don't want to learn patience. We want everything NOW! We want God to come down from heaven, and to kill our bosses when they make us angry. We want instant justice. We want God to miraculously end cancer for everyone. Because it hasn't happened, we discredit God. What about all of the testimonies about people who were miraculously healed? Doctors who don't even believe in the power of Jesus Christ will attest that they have seen diseases miraculously disappear.

Just like "slumps," people will see what they want to. It's not any different from the Old Testament Jewish perspective on Jesus. Early prophecy said that Israel would be restored by the Messiah. He would save the people. The Jews were looking for what they thought the Messiah should look like. They wanted God to address their situation the way they saw fit. They wanted a king that would drive out the Romans, and rebuild the nation into its former, glorious self. Jesus wasn't the valiant, land-conquering king they had hoped for. Instead, He was a messiah that would save the Jews and Gentiles alike from spiritual death. God was working on a bigger scale. The Jews wanted a fighter; instead they got a peacemaker. The prophets before Jesus spoke of Him being a victorious king that would restore peace. During the time of Jesus' ministry, Rome was heavily oppressing the Jewish nation. The Jews' afflictions made them focus on what they wanted to see. They were so overjoyed about the prophecy of the Messiah, because they wanted to get from up under Rome's thumb. So to them, Jesus was a joke.

Here He was, giving His life for the same people that called Him phony. Sounds like us today, right? Jesus had come as a servant, suffering for our sin to establish His kingdom. He declared in John 18:36 that "My kingdom is not of this world. If My kingdom were of this world, My servants would fight, so that I should not be delivered to the Jews; but now My kingdom is not from here." He fulfilled the prophecy, just not the way they wanted Him to do so. So ask yourself, has God fulfilled promises in your life that you haven't given Him credit for? Is He still teaching you lessons that you refuse to learn? Are you calling those times that He molds you "slumps"? If so, stop reading and acknowledge Him right now! Tell God thank you for His nurturing heart toward us. We have to go back to the initial point of this book, and never forget it.

We have to SEARCH our THOUGHTS, because this is WAR.

We battle with the enemy every day. We battle with sin every day. We battle our thoughts every day. We battle, we battle, we battle. The quicker you understand the war tactics the devil is using on you, the quicker you can be set free.

Everything written in this book works together. There are many other tactics the enemy uses that weren't annotated in this book. You have to prepare yourself for success. Somehow we have adopted this idea of God that makes us feel like He should be getting rid of sin on earth at this moment. We think He should be keeping such things like death and torture from happening. Actually, He did. Jesus died for us. That's how much He loves us. That's how God changed our present world. He told us of the New Jerusalem in the book of Revelations.

Let me give you a proper perspective on this. Envision yourself on a team, playing in the NBA finals. It's game seven. Before the game, you might be nervous. In your brain, you visualize all the things, good and bad, that could happen. When you finally get on the court, the game is intense. By halftime, your team is down by twenty points. You go into the locker room extremely upset. At Pre-game shootaround, you thought about all of the components of the game. You were worried that you might miss your shots. You were thinking about the competition, and the possibility of losing. All these things you contemplated before they occurred. You stressed over them as if they were tangible, even though all your thoughts were hypothetical. Now that you are losing, you don't care about any of those things. You just want to win now, and you'll do whatever to make that happen.

What if the coach came into the locker room during half-time and told you that, in the end, your team would come back and win by one point? You didn't believe him, though. You still worried as you played, instead of just going out and balling. As the last buzzer went off, you noticed that your coach was right. You looked up at the scoreboard and contemplated that he had predicted your one point victory before it happened. Now looking back, if you knew your coach's words were going to be prophetically true, would you have worried the entire time? Would you have enjoyed the moment more since you knew the outcome? That's what God intended when He gave us the knowledge of His existence and things to come. He gave us a slight glimpse into the future so we wouldn't get so caught up in this world. I know death hurts, but only because the enemy makes you feel that way. Under God, death and birth are the same thing. To a believer that loves the Lord, we came from God, and to God we will go back. So there is no pain attached to death for us.

When my parents do pass away from here, I will mourn them. The blessing behind it all, though, is that I will see them again. The next time I see them, we will be with our Lord and Savior Jesus Christ. This next time will be for all eternity. I will never lose them again. How awesome is that! It's like we're all at the airport looking for our flights. This world is the terminal. So many of you are complaining about the conditions of the airport terminal, and we haven't even made it on the plane. The glory is in the trip and our final destination. Quit looking at the trash in the corner. It's an airport terminal, what do you expect? This is life. Again, what do you expect? Don't be so down about this corrupt world, but instead, be filled with joy about eternity with Jesus. God gave that gift card to all of us. It's sad that only a few of us cashed it in. Don't allow Satan to keep you from God's love for an eternity. Whatever sins or unbelief you hold toward God are not worth it. I'm serious.

If you do decide to accept Jesus as your Lord and Savior, don't get discouraged. We all have our own walk with God. The same way when a woman has two kids, and they act totally different, so are we in the body of Christ. We are all made uniquely. That's why certain temptations that affect you, might not affect me. It would be worthless for me to try and act like another Christian. So don't mimic the walk of your brother and sisters in Christ; just mimic Jesus. Men and women will fall right before your eyes. We are mortal. Jesus gave us the proper example. Just seek Him with expectancy. We need to acknowledge the devil for who he is, but his power stops there. He has no true control: you make the decisions. He only can play mind games with you. We have to let go and grow. We do that by keeping our eyes on the Lord. The people are His problem. Judgment is His authority.

I can't make you read my book and change. What I can do is pray for you. I also can work on myself. That's what I have control over. That starts with me developing a relationship with the Lord and speaking with Him constantly. Through our communion, the Holy Spirit will show me God's way. I will begin to see who I am beyond the lies of Satan. I will begin to see who I am in the eyes of the Lord. No situation fully dictates who we are as men and women. We are children of God. Period! Luke 4:18 says, "The Spirit of the Lord is upon Me, because He has appointed Me to preach the gospel to the poor; He has sent Me to heal the brokenhearted, to proclaim liberty to the captives and recovery of sight to the blind, to set at liberty those who are oppressed." That's our mission. "Our" includes you, the individual reading this book. Don't let Satan make you quit on your life, and keep you from the love we all experience in Jesus. It's like nothing I can describe. I'm dead honest. It's tangible. He speaks to me. He chastises me. He cares for and protects me. You can experience Him as well.

Romans 10:9 states, "That if you confess with your mouth the Lord Jesus and believe in your heart that God has raised Him from the dead, you will be saved." That's it. Just say the words, "I love you Jesus. I believe in you Jesus. I believe you rose from the dead, and I want to follow you to eternity." If you meant what you said, then I will see you in heaven. So until that time when we will meet in the celestial skies, I leave you with this:

2 Corinthians 5:17
"Therefore, if anyone is in Christ, he is a
new creation; old things have passed away;
behold all things have become new."

You might feel the same, but you are not. The Holy Spirit now dwells in you. The enemy will try to persuade you back to his side. He will tell you many lies. It's on you to disregard them with the Word of God. Be strong, my brothers and sisters in Jesus. Walk valiantly to the cross. ALWAYS BE A SOLDIER!

CPSIA information can be obtained at www.ICGtesting.com
Printed in the USA
BVOW04s1334290714

360871BV00002B/2/P